Keeping Christ in Christmas

Steve Russo

HARVEST HOUSE PUBLISHERS
Eugene, Oregon 97402

Cover by Terry Dugan Design, Minneapolis, Minnesota

KEEPING CHRIST IN CHRISTMAS

Copyright © 1999 by Steve Russo
Published by Harvest House Publishers
Eugene, Oregon 97402

Library of Congress Cataloging-in-Publication Data
    Russo, Steve, 1953–
        Keeping Christ in Christmas / Steve Russo.
            p. cm.
        Includes bibliographical references.
        ISBN 0-7369-0166-3
        1. Christmas.   I. Title.
    GT4985.R87   1999
    394.2663—dc21   99-21978
                                                                          CIP

Printed in the United States of America

99 00 01 02 03 04 / BC / 10 9 8 7 6 5 4 3 2 1

Acknowledgments

This book is truly the result of many people working in close cooperation.

Where would I be without all my friends at Harvest House Publishers? They have earned my appreciation for believing in the potential of this project. In particular, I am grateful to Bob Hawkins Jr., LaRae Weikert, Carolyn McCready, Chip MacGregor, Betty Fletcher, Julie McKinney and Teresa Evenson.

Many thanks to the Russo Team Office staff—Janet Graley and Antoinette Buma—for taking on extra responsibilities so I could concentrate on writing this volume.

A special word of appreciation to Dr. Robert Saucy, from Talbot Theological Seminary, for giving the project a review through the eyes of a theologian. I learned much from him while a seminary student and continue to appreciate his gifts and input into my life.

My most special thanks, as always, goes to my family. My wife Tami has again proven to be a great source of encouragement and support. My children Tony, Kati, and Gabi, have been affected by my time spent writing, however they have been nothing less than encouraging the whole time.

Ultimately, my hope is that this book will honor my Lord and Savior Jesus Christ, and that it will help many people remember the "reason for the season."

Contents

PART I:
WHAT IS THE HISTORY
OF CHRISTMAS?

1. *Christmas: In the Beginning* **9**
2. *Santa Claus, Mistletoe, and Candy Canes* **21**
3. *Christmas Around the World* **47**

PART II:
WHAT HAPPENED TO THE INNOCENCE
OF CHRISTMAS?

4. *The Christmas Rush* **71**
5. *Whatever Happened to Christmas Vacation?* **79**
6. *Touched by an Angel* **91**

PART III:
WHAT'S A CHRISTIAN
TO DO?

7. *A Look at the Book* **103**
8. *Parenting in a Consumer Culture* **109**
9. *How to Keep Christ in Christmas* **119**
10. *The Promise of Christmas* **133**
11. *Where Do I Go From Here?* **141**

Part One:

What Is
the History
of Christmas?

1

Christmas:
In the Beginning

It's easy to think that Christmas has been celebrated since the very first eve of Jesus' birth, when angels proclaimed His arrival on the plains of Bethlehem. However, this is not the case. Historically, Christmas has endured occasional tribulation, careful scrutiny, and even attempted eradication along the way. The creation of Christmas celebrations as we know them did not happen overnight. Christmas trees and family gatherings and holiday decorations are relatively recent developments. The celebration as we know it was shaped by many people and cultures over a period of centuries, and did not catch on in popular culture until the middle of the nineteenth century. The holiday has been influenced by everything from Roman festivals to Queen Victoria's wedding. But most of the elements of the traditional Christmas story have their origin in the New Testament books of Matthew and Luke. Together these two books give us an incredible account of the birth of Jesus.

Before we learn more about that first Christmas and how early Christians celebrated the holiday, let's examine the predictions concerning His birth. Then we'll look closely at that very first Christmas through the eyes of Luke. It's an incredible true story that is still impacting lives centuries later.

The Predictions of His Birth

The Old Testament prophecies concerning the incarnation of Christ — Jesus coming in the flesh — focused primarily on three things. First was the manner in which He would be born. Isaiah 7:14 prophesied that a virgin would bear a son who would be called Immanuel, which means "God with us." The New Testament fulfillment of this prophecy occurs in Matthew 1:23: "The virgin will be with child and will give birth to a son, and they will call him Immanuel, which means God with us."

Second was the prediction regarding the place where Jesus would be born. Micah 5:2 identified the birthplace of Christ as Bethlehem — a small, seemingly insignificant town. And Matthew 2:6 reveals the fulfillment of this prophecy 700 years later: "But you, Bethlehem, in the land of Judah, are by no means least among the rulers of Judah; for out of you will come a ruler who will be the shepherd of my people Israel." Most religious leaders, at the time of Christ's birth, believed in a literal fulfillment of Old Testament prophecy, and therefore believed the Messiah would be born in Bethlehem. Ironically, when Jesus was born, these same religious leaders became His greatest enemies. When the Messiah for whom they had been waiting finally came, they didn't even recognize Him.

Third is an important truth about Jesus — He is both God and man. In Isaiah 9:6, the prophet foretold the union of God and humanity in Christ, explaining that a child would be born, but that His character would be such that He would be called "Mighty God." Why did God send His Son in the likeness of sinful flesh? The Bible gives several answers to that question, including: to reveal God to us (John 1:18), to provide an example for our lives (I Peter 2:21), to provide an effective sacrifice for sin (Hebrews 10:1-10), and to destroy the works of the devil (I John 3:8). God took on the limitations of humanity so He could live and die for the salvation of all who believe in Him.

The First Christmas

The book of Luke offers some incredible details about the very first Christmas. The author begins by describing current events of the day. Palestine was under the rule of the Roman Empire. Cæsar Augustus, the adopted son of Julius Caesar, was in charge. Not satisfied with being king, he chose the title "Augustus"—"exalted one"—in an attempt to make himself a god. Caesar then signed a tax bill that the whole world would be taxed, needing money to pay for an army in order to control his vast empire and provide for his luxurious lifestyle.

In order to collect the tax and keep good records, the government forced Joseph to make a 70-mile trip just to pay his taxes. His fiancée, who had to go with him, was going to have a baby any minute. The city was crowded, and when they arrived in Bethlehem the couple couldn't even find a place to stay. They finally took refuge in a stable, according to Luke 2:

> While they were there, the time came for the baby to be born, and she gave birth to her firstborn, a son. She wrapped him in clothes and placed him in a manger, because there was no room for them in the inn.
>
> And there were shepherds living out in the fields nearby, keeping watch over their flocks at night. An angel of the Lord appeared to them, and the glory of the Lord shone around them, and they were terrified. But the angel said to them, Do not be afraid. I will bring you good news of great joy that will be for all the people. Today in the town of David a Savior has been born to you; he is Christ the Lord. This will be a sign to you: You will find a baby wrapped in cloths and lying in a manger.
>
> Suddenly a great company of the heavenly host appeared with the angel, praising God and saying, "Glory to God in the highest and on earth peace to men on whom his favor rests."
>
> —Luke 2:6-14

What a birth announcement! The shepherds were terrified, but their fear turned to joy as the angels announced Christ's coming. They ran to see the baby; then they spread the word.

The story of Jesus' birth resounds with music that has inspired composers for 2,000 years. The angels' song in Luke 2:14— "Glory to God in the highest and on earth peace to men on whom his favor rests"—is an all-time favorite. It's the basis for contemporary choral works, traditional Christmas carols, and ancient liturgical chants.

Many people have wondered when Jesus was born, but the Bible doesn't offer the exact date of Christ's birth. We do know, however, that it could not have been in the dead of winter. As Luke knew, shepherds would not have been roaming the hills at night during the winter with their sheep. Most scholars agree that Jesus was likely born in the spring or summer in the year 4 B.C.[1] Bible scholar J. Vernon McGee says the date of His birth is irrelevant, just as the day upon which He was crucified is irrelevant. We don't need to know the exact day He was born; the important thing is that He was born.

And while our first impression of Jesus is as a baby lying in a manger, that must not be our last impression. The Christ child in a manger makes a great Christmas picture, but this helpless, tiny baby lived an incredible life, died for us, ascended into heaven, and is coming back for the second time. When he returns it will not be as a humble carpenter but as the King of kings.

Early Celebrations of Christmas

If Christmas celebrations had begun the very year Jesus was born, the holiday would be nearing its 2000th anniversary. However, early Christians did not observe the festival of Christ's birth, nor did they attach the same importance to His birth that they did to His death and resurrection. Christmas had to wait more than 300 years to be celebrated in any meaningful way.

The early days of Christianity saw great growth partnered with terrible persecution. For the first 200 years of the Church,

Christians endured imprisonment and death at the hands of the Roman Empire.

When Emperor Constantine came to power in 306, the prevailing religion in the Roman Empire was Mithraism—the worship of the Persian sun-god. But as a result of Constantine's conversion, Christianity became the state religion. Public money was used to build churches. In fact, it was Constantine who commissioned the construction of the Church of the Nativity, on a spot in Bethlehem assumed to be the exact birthplace of Jesus. By the end of the fourth century, most other forms of worship had been banned and Christianity was spreading rapidly across the Roman Empire.

There is only one record of Christmas being celebrated on December 25 in the early Church, and that was in Antioch (modern-day Turkey) in the middle of the second century. There is no record of it being celebrated on that date in Rome until the year 336. A few years later, in A.D. 350, Pope Julius I declared December 25 the official date of Christ's birth, and in 529 Emperor Justinian declared Christmas a public holiday. Later, at the Council of Tours in 567, legislation was passed that made Advent a period of preparation and fasting.

The December date for Christmas was not arbitrary but was a calculated decision that reflected the importance of winter solstice festivals for the non-Christian cultures in Europe and Asia. To abolish these festivals in favor of only Christian forms of celebration would have been political suicide, so it became clear to church leaders early on that rather than trying to beat the non-Christians, it would be wiser to join them. Thus the Church incorporated deep-rooted pagan traditions into Christmas worship and celebration.

Ancient peoples believed that the days grew shorter in December because the sun was leaving them. Some even believed that the sun was dying, and festivals held right before the December 21 winter solstice featured ceremonies designed to pacify the sun and convince it to return. After the solstice—the shortest day of the year—the days got longer again and magnificent celebrations were held in honor of the sun's return. Besides the idea of the physical return of the sun, there also were underlying themes of rebirth, light, and harvest. Although the basic concept of the festival was common to all lands, each area had its unique celebration. The tradition that had the greatest impact on the Christmas celebration was the Roman Saturnalia.

The Saturnalia was observed December 17–24 and was a combined celebration of several different events, among them Saturn's triumph over Jupiter. During the festivities all businesses closed down except those involved in food service and entertainment. No one else worked, slaves and masters became equal, and there was much feasting, dancing, gambling, and partying. Candles were used as decorations to scare away the darkness and celebrate the sun and light. There was the giving of gifts, done in honor of the goddess of vegetation, Strenia. People believed that in time of darkness and winter, it was important to praise someone who had a hand in the harvest. Baked goods and produce were exchanged, and as time progressed, other types of gifts became favorable.

The earliest of the Church's numerous battles over the less-than-reverent nature of some solstice celebrations resulted in a compromise. The decision was made to adapt certain pagan symbols and ceremonies to the Christmas tradition. Both popular and church interests were therefore satisfied. People got to keep their time of fun, and the church ensured that the birth of Christ would be celebrated with due honor. Many elements of the old festivals remained, while others were transformed to honor Jesus' birth. Some of the elements retained are still popular today, including greenery, candles, feasting, yule logs, singing, and tree decorating. But why celebrate December 25, rather than the actual time of the solstice—December 21 or 22?

The use of December 25 was a remnant of the Mithraic religion, a dominant religion of the Roman Empire with close similarities to Christianity. Mithra, the god of light and wisdom, was said to have been born from a rock on December 25. Symbolizing the sun, Mithra was naturally a big part of solstice festivals, and his birth was celebrated as a major holiday by his followers. In the third century, before Constantine became emperor, Emperor Aurelian declared December 25 the "Day of the Invincible Sun." When Constantine converted to Christianity, remnants of his old religion remained throughout his empire.

For many people, incorporating Mithraic rites into the celebration of Christmas was easy to justify. Jesus represents life, triumph over death and darkness, and restored hope and light. So rather than celebrating the sun, people would be celebrating the Son of God. In other words, the birth of Christ *replaced* the birth of the sun as cause for celebration.

Historic Celebrations of Christmas

The invasions of the Roman Empire that began in the fifth century brought the Nordic and Germanic peoples into contact with Christianity and therefore into contact with Christmas. In northern and western Europe, people had their own solstice customs, which were to be incorporated into Christmas. Evergreens were used as a symbol of life, and what we would call the yule log was lit at this time of darkness to symbolize the eventual triumph of light over the darkness. The festive meal was the boar's head, and these customs have been presented in centuries-old carols, including wassail songs, holly carols, and boar's head carols that are still sung today.

As Christianity made its way across Europe, Christmas celebrations came with it. At the end of the sixth century, the pope told Emperor Augustine to change the midwinter yule festival into a Christmas celebration. Augustine was also instructed to include any of the customs from the festival that could be found to contain Christian significance. It was a time-tested strategy, and it worked—Christmas came to Germany in 813 by the Synod of Mainz, and to Norway in the mid-900s by King Hakon the Good. By the end of the ninth century, Christmas was celebrated all over

Europe with trees, gifts, feasts, and lights. Anything that held significance for the old religions was either altered to fit into a Christian context or tossed aside.

Today Christmas is celebrated on December 25 by Catholics and Protestants alike, but many eastern European churches refuse to observe this date, choosing instead to combine Epiphany and Nativity celebrations on January 6. Originally "Epiphany" marked the manifestation of God to the world in the form of Jesus. Later, when the Romans began introducing Christianity to the West, they changed the notion of Epiphany to represent the day the Wise Men came and presented their gifts to Jesus. Tradition marks this date on January 6, thus the date of the Eastern Orthodox Christmas celebration.

The height of Christmas rowdiness and extravagance was achieved in medieval England after 1066. People would do their partying at church by donning masks and costumes, gambling on the altar, and singing off-color songs. There also were godly caroling and Nativity plays that people participated in, and the celebration stretched for twelve full days.

Christmas seemed to reach a new height of royal excess in 1377. In that year King Richard II of England had a Christmas feast for more than 10,000 people (Historical records do not indicate whether the 2000 cooks employed at the feast enjoyed the holiday!) In 1533 King Henry VIII declared himself the supreme head of the Church of England and one of the responsibilities he took on was the power to regulate religious holidays, including Christmas. Henry then preceded to rival Richard in yuletide extravagance. Under his rule Christmas became a national obsession. Christmas celebrations were filled with dancing, plays, food, and widespread carousing—a tradition carried on by his daughter Elizabeth I.

Some members of the clergy were not happy with the way in which Christ's birth was being remembered. Aside from the games and gluttony, they were concerned with the notion of observing Jesus' birth as if He were just a person rather than God in the flesh. They argued that these celebrations should be more spiritual, and the more Christmas became established in the customs and hearts of the people, the more the clergy worried. Reservations regarding the pagan elements began to surface again, and some church officials even questioned the prudence of having allowed them in the first place. With the Protestant Reformation, these objections acquired the support of an organized power.

Beginning in 1517 with the posting of Martin Luther's 95 theses on the chapel door of Wittenberg University, the Reformation movement attacked religious feasts and saints' days as corrupt practices. Christmas was outlawed in 1583 in Scotland. Puritans and Protestants in England condemned the drinking, gluttony, and partying associated with Christmas celebrations. Some even argued for all pagan customs to be done away with. By this time, most Protestants observed Christmas as a quiet day of reflection. Yet the Puritans did not observe it at all and by the middle of the seventeenth century, the holiday was under heavy fire.

England entered its Commonwealth period, ruled by Oliver Cromwell and the Puritans. The government eventually issued official policies outlawing all religious festivals. One such law was issued in 1644 regarding public Christmas celebrations:

> *Whereas some doubts have been raised whether the next Feast shall be celebrated because it falleth on the day which, heretofore, was usually called the Feast of Nativity of our Saviour, the lords and commons do order and ordain that public notice be given, that the Feast appointed to be kept on the last Wednesday in every month, ought to be observed until it is otherwise ordered by both houses; and that this day particularly is to be kept with the same solemn humiliation because it may call to remembrance our sins and the sins of our forefathers, who have turned this Feast, pretending the memory of Christ, into an extreme forgetfulness of him, by giving liberty to carnal and sensual delights.*

The period of the Puritan reign was filled with similar laws, some even more strict than this one. In the initial days of these ordinances, people tried to disobey and there was even some rioting. But gradually the government won out. Christmas became an outlaw, and so did those who attempted to celebrate it in any way. Churches were locked on December 25, and the singing of carols was considered illegal. The Puritans meant to banish the excessiveness and pagan roots from the country and the hearts of the people, and they came very close to succeeding until the Restoration came along.

Christmas was legalized again when the monarchy returned to power in 1660, led by Charles II. People were ecstatic because the holiday could be observed freely again and with the lifting of the formal bans instituted by the Puritans and with the good will of the leaders, Christmas seemed to be ready for a comeback in England. But it was not to be. At the outset of the Restoration, the holiday was only a shadow of what it once was. The pagan excesses were not the only things lost to the Puritan purge—so was the Christmas spirit. It seemed to have left the hearts and minds of the people.

Even though the Puritans had been dethroned, much of their philosophy still imbued the Church. Christmas may have been legalized, but it still was opposed by some powerful members of the clergy, and this kept the holiday from making much of a public recovery in the latter part of the seventeenth century.

Modern Celebrations of Christmas

As the years passed and the time of Puritan rule faded into distant memory, the attitude towards Christmas actually got worse. Due to the continuing resistance from some members of the clergy and a changing social climate, by the time the Industrial Revolution began, all thoughts seemed to turn toward work, money, and progress. In this new fast-paced atmosphere, there appeared to be no room left for holidays. The mindless greed and soul-crushing poverty were epitomized in Charles Dickens' literary indictment *A Christmas Carol*. People had a hard time finding much to celebrate during this time in English history.

However, throughout that period there were small, quiet groups of people who kept the holiday alive in their homes and hearts.

While public Christmas celebrations in England faced both adverse social conditions and religious objections, the Germans were keeping the flame alive. They were enjoying an expansive and marvelous Christmas tradition that had been building up over the centuries. It's quite probable the American love affair with Christmas that started in the late nineteenth and early twentieth centuries—so influential in how the whole world observes the holiday—would never have happened if not for the enthusiastic Christmas-loving German immigrants. The German people have long embraced the concept of keeping the spirit of Christmas alive in one's mind, spirit, and heart, then turning those feelings outward in mass celebration. The German Christmas celebration was one of gingerbread houses, trees, feasts, cookies, and carols. Most of all, the German Christmas was one of childhood joy and wonder. The German people have had an enormous part to play in shaping the modern Christmas celebration we know and love. One of the early beneficiaries of the German Christmas spirit was Victorian England.

In 1837, Victoria assumed the throne at the tender age of eighteen. Three years later she married Prince Albert, who was of German descent. Prince Albert brought with him to England many of the wonderful Christmas traditions of his homeland. Very quickly Christmas became a special occasion for the Royal Family. Their celebration emphasized the importance of family closeness, a greater appreciation of children, decorations, and a festive holiday meal.

In 1841, Prince Albert introduced the first Christmas tree to Windsor Castle. Since Victoria and her family enjoyed enormous popularity, much of what they did was widely emulated. Over the course of Victoria's reign, the tide turned. Christmas once again played an important part in English life. The Christmas card was created during the Victorian Era. Carols got their biggest boost since they had been legalized under Charles II. Caroling became popular in churches and homes, and groups of carolers roamed the streets. Most of the images we have today of outdoor carolers are from this period, as is the idea of giving and concern for others, especially those in need.

Without a doubt, the Victorian Christmas dinner menu is the one most people envision as "classic." The dinner included turkey, goose or roast beef, mincemeat pie, Yorkshire and plum puddings, wassail, and eggnog. The custom of giving gifts on Christmas Day did not come about until the last few decades of the nineteenth century. Before that, England adhered to the old Roman tradition of waiting until New Year's day. Eventually Christmas became the day for giving gifts, and it was England's turn to borrow from America, where Santa Claus became the model for England's "Father Christmas."

By the beginning of the twentieth century, Christmas had been fully established as a holiday in England. The Victorians had helped to mold Christmas tradition that would forever alter the way Christmas would be celebrated in England, America, and many parts of the world.

2

Santa Claus, Mistletoe, and Candy Canes

Many adults remember growing up with the adventure of leaving cookies and milk out on Christmas Eve for Santa Claus. They would wake up the next morning to find the snack gone and presents left under the tree and in their stockings. Where did these traditions come from? This chapter will look at the origins of all our favorite Christmas traditions.

Bells and Noisemakers

In pagan times, bells and other noisemakers were believed to frighten away evil spirits. Bell-ringing activities were a serious and often rowdy part of the midwinter solstice festivals. As late as the 1890s, children in the United States thought of Christmas and noisemakers as almost synonymous. (The demise of the small, wildly popular "Christmas firecracker" probably had as much to do with care of parental eardrums as with safety concerns.) However, bells—especially church bells—remain a staple of the holiday celebration. Their ringing serves as an unmistakable herald of the arrival of the Christmas season.

The Boar's Head

English legend has it that a philosophy student once fended off the attack of a wild boar by choking the animal with a book on Aristotle. Once the boar was dead, the student cut off his head to remove the book, and brought the head back to his college, where he and his friends had a feast. Thus began the tradition of every English household having a boar's head for Christmas dinner.

A more likely explanation is that the custom is another remnant of pagan times. The German god Frey, in some places, was considered responsible for the well-being of livestock. Because Frey was symbolized by the boar, often a boar was sacrificed in hopes of a prosperous spring herd. Like many other popular Christmas traditions in medieval England, the boar's head eventually became impractical and died out. Boars became increasingly difficult to track down, and were dangerous to catch when found. In addition, the week's work of preparation and cooking required was better suited to a well-staffed castle kitchen than that of a normal home. Gradually the boar's head was replaced by more familiar meats like pork, turkey, roast beef, and goose.

Candles

Candles were an important source of heat and light in the time of darkness surrounding the winter solstice. Romans lit candles during Saturnalia to convince the sun to shine once again and ward off evil. From this early pagan start, the candle has gone on to become an essential part of Christmas lighting, both at home and in church services.

Candles are used during Advent to mark the days before the coming of Christmas. For Christians they symbolize Christ Himself, the Light of the world. In Victorian times, candles came to represent concern and good will for the poor and needy during the holiday season. They often were placed in windows over the twelve days of Christmas as a sign to needy passersby that warmth and shelter could be found within.

Candles were the preferred means of lighting Christmas trees for many years. The first string of electric Christmas tree lights were sold in 1903. However, only the wealthy could afford them, and only those with indoor electric outlets could use them. Most people continued to follow the earlier (and more dangerous) tradition of fixing small lighted candles to the branches of the tree. Although replaced in windows and on trees for the most part, real candles are still used in church celebrations and caroling ceremonies.

Candy Canes

The legend of the candy cane claims that a candymaker in Indiana wanted to use his product as a witness for his faith. He began with a stick of pure white candy, symbolizing the virgin birth and the sinless nature of Jesus. The candy was made in the shape of a "J" to represent the precious name of Jesus, who came to earth as our Savior. It would also represent the staff of the "Good Shepherd," with which He reaches down into the ditches of the world to lift up fallen lambs who have gone astray.

Thinking the candy somewhat plain, the candymaker stained it with red stripes to represent the scourging Jesus received. The large red stripe was for the blood shed by the Lord on the cross, our promise of eternal life.

Unfortunately, the candy became known as the candy cane—a meaningless decorative treat seen at Christmastime. But the deeper meaning is still there for those who seek the truth.

Carols

Perhaps no other holiday is as closely associated with music and singing as Christmas. Traditionally, the singing of carols at Christmastime commemorates the song the angels sang when they appeared to the shepherds at Bethlehem to announce the birth of Jesus.

The present-day meaning of "carol" is far removed from its original one. A carol once was a secular dance that could be performed at any time of the year. People formed a ring, holding hands, and as they circled around, they joined together in singing a song. Because the configuration of the individuals in this "ring dance" reminded onlookers of a coronet, or *corolla* in Latin, they called it a "carol." The name was later transferred from the dance to the song itself.

During the Middle Ages, groups of serenaders called "waits" would travel from house to house singing ancient carols and spreading holiday cheer. The word "carol" came to mean "song of joy," and the English looked upon their carols as a link with Britain's ancient past. Because of their ties to pagan ritual, English carols often emphasized material pleasure—"The Boar's Head in Hand," "The Holly and Ivy," and "Here We Go a-Wassailing" are all examples of this concept.

The oldest carol in manuscript form was written by Norman French and describes the Nativity. It was printed in the fourteenth century, although it was written prior to that. By the sixteenth century, carols had become a very popular feature of the Christmas celebration, though they were sung only in church, and only by the clergy and bishop. However, the carols caught the people's imagination and soon were sung in public places and on the streets in joyful celebration of Christ's birth.

In Canada, French missionaries were responsible for what is thought to be the first Christmas carol written in the New World. It was entitled "Jesous Ahatonna" and was composed by a Jesuit priest, Father Brebeuf. This carol was preserved by tradition for approximately 150 years at the Laureate Mission, until it finally was written down by Father de Villeneuve. The melody, an old French tune called "Une jeune puccelle," is similar to "God Rest Ye Merry Gentlemen."

Most of the popular old carols we sing today were written in the nineteenth century. American poets and composers wrote carols that have become fixtures of our holiday celebration. John

Henry Hopkins, a New England clergyman and musician, composed music for his poem "We Three Kings," and Edward Hamilton Sears, a Unitarian minister in Massachusetts, wrote the text of "It Came Upon a Midnight Clear" in 1849.

Christmas Animals

Besides the relatively recent addition of reindeer, there are a few other animals that have been linked to Christmas. Goats, camels, horses, sheep, and donkeys all have been associated with the biblical story of the Nativity. Even though sheep are the only ones explicitly mentioned, most representations of the manger scene include some, if not all, of the other animals.

In some countries the Camel of Jesus brings gifts to the children. In Hamlet, Shakespeare mentions the legendary "bird of dawning," which was believed to sing the whole night through at Christmastime. There are other legends told about animals receiving the power to speak on the night Christ was born. Some traditions say that every year between Christmas Eve and Christmas morning, this power returns and animals can talk to us. Still another legend has oxen kneeling every Christmas Eve at midnight.

The Christmas Bonus

The first Christmas bonus was instituted in 1899 by department store owner F.W. Woolworth. Going by the assumption that happy workers are productive and reliable workers, Woolworth gave a bonus of $5 to each employee for each year of service, not to exceed $25—quite a sum of money in those days! (The idea of giving employees Christmas Day off was not observed until 1875. Up to that time, workers were expected to report to the job as usual, unless the holiday fell on a Sunday.)

The holiday bonus has a counterpart in the Christmas tip generally given to service workers, mail carriers, and others. Both are outgrowths of the English custom of giving to the needy on Boxing Day—the day after Christmas.

Christmas Cards

John Calcott Horsley is given the distinction of having created the first printed Christmas card. Horsley printed his card in 1843 for Sir Henry Cole, the friend who had given him the idea. His card looked a lot like a postcard, consisting of three panels. The center panel depicted a typical English family enjoying the holiday. (This particular panel caused some controversy because it showed a child drinking wine.) The other panels pictured acts of charity, an important part of the Victorian Christmas spirit. That first card's inscription read "Merry Christmas and a Happy New Year to You." One thousand copies of the card were printed, selling for a shilling apiece.

Among the Victorians, Christmas cards soon became a popular means of sending holiday greetings, and most of the cards had no religious bent to them. In 1840, the onset of the "penny post" made it affordable for most people to send these greetings by mail. The invention of the steam press made mass production of Christmas cards possible, and since the British postal service delivered on Christmas Day, that's when most people received their cards.

The firm of Marcus Ward & Company popularized the Christmas card in America. A German-born printer and lithographer, Louis Prang, also helped build the card's reputation. Prang first used his talents with Christmas cards in 1875 when he designed and printed them in his shop in Roxbury, Massachusetts. He created colored lithographs (or "chromos" as he called them) in eight colors. Prang's cards pictured Nativity scenes, nature scenes, family scenes, and eventually Santa Claus. His marketing techniques, in addition to the beauty of his cards, ensured their popularity. Prang held contests all over the country, enticing public interest by offering unique prizes for the best card designs. Prang's cards sold very well until America began importing cheaper cards from German manufacturers.

Christmas Rose

The legend of the Christmas Rose comes from a modern children's story. The legend claims there was a young girl who wanted to worship the baby Jesus, but felt that she could not because she had no present to give him. Upset, the girl began to cry. As her tears fell to the ground, they created a bush bearing a beautiful white rose, which she then gave to Christ.

Christmas Seals

Christmas, like Easter, has a special seal dedicated to helping the needy. The Christmas Seal was created in Denmark in 1903 by postal worker Einar Holboell, who felt there should be a special stamp to benefit tuberculosis sufferers. Each year since then, the seal has had a new design. The first seal was printed in 1904 with a picture of Queen Louise of Denmark, and more than four million were sold. Sweden followed suit that same year, and Norway had its own seals by 1905.

The Christmas Seal owes its popularity in America primarily to Emily Bissell, state secretary of the Red Cross in Wilmington, Delaware. Word of the seal's success in Scandinavia had spread to America, and Bissell wanted to use a seal to help keep a local tuberculosis treatment center open. The first American seal, designed by Bissell in 1907, depicted a cross, holly, and the words "Merry Christmas and Happy New Year." By 1908 the Christmas Seal was circulating across the country by a variety of charities. In 1919 the National Tuberculosis Association—later the American Lung Association—became the seal's sole beneficiary. The double-barred Cross of Lorraine became the seal's signature component that same year.

Christmas Stamps

Christmas stamps are issued each season to give the mail some holiday spirit. The stamps do not benefit any organization, but each year the United States Postal Service features different secular or religious scenes. Actually, the first Christmas stamps were printed in Canada in 1898. The United States did not start printing them until 1962. A Christmas stamp depicting a reproduction of the Renaissance painting "The Adoration of the Shepherds" by Italian painter Giorgione was the most popular stamp in US history until the Elvis Presley stamp came along. Over one billion of the Giorgione Christmas stamps were printed.

Christmas Trees

Most people cannot imagine celebrating the Christmas holiday without a tree sitting in their living room. Like many other things that we associate with Christmas, the tree is a relatively recent innovation in America. Apparently the decorated Christmas tree had no broad popularity in colonial America. The tradition, followed by German immigrants for many years, did not catch on in other parts of society until the 1830s. Some historians believe that the Hessians, defeated by George Washington in the Battle of Trenton in 1776, may have been observing the holiday in the tradition of their homeland by setting lighted candles on the boughs of the tree. The light from their trees gave away their positions and led to their defeat.

According to legend, St. Boniface, who helped organize the Christian church in France and Germany during the mid-700s, was responsible for the first Christmas tree. On one Christmas Eve, St. Boniface was traveling through the forest and happened upon a group of people gathered around an oak tree, preparing to sacrifice a child to the god Thor. In protest of this act, St. Boniface destroyed the oak, and planted a fir tree in its place. St. Boniface told the people that this was the Tree of Life, representing Jesus.

Another old legend says that when Christ was born, all the trees bloomed and brought forth fruit, despite the harsh winter. The grand trees came forward to worship the Lord—except one tiny fir tree that was embarrassed by its stature. Then the Lord came down and lit the fir tree's branches, making it sparkle, and it was no longer ashamed.

The most popular Christmas tree legend has to do with Martin Luther. The story claims that one Christmas Eve, as Luther was ambling through the forest, he became enraptured by the beauty of the starlight playing off the branches of evergreen trees. Luther then chopped down a tree, brought it home, and lit it with candles in an effort to duplicate the scene for his family. (Because of Luther's supposed association with the Christmas tree, strict Roman Catholic inhabitants of southern Germany would not have trees in their homes. In the nineteenth century, when news of the custom's popularity in America traveled overseas, Christmas trees finally made their way into German Roman Catholic homes.)

As fascinating as these legends are, most experts believe the truth behind the Christmas tree's popularity is much less impressive. In Europe during the fourteenth and fifteenth centuries, pine trees were used as part of the miracle plays performed in front of the cathedrals at Christmastime. The plays detailed the birth and fall of humanity, then its salvation through the death and resurrection of Christ. Decorated with apples, the pine trees symbolized the Tree of the Knowledge of Good and Evil in the Garden of Eden.

Later the church banned such plays, but the tradition of this *Paradeisbaum*, or "Paradise Tree," was kept alive in individual homes. People began decorating these trees with wafers to represent the Eucharist. As time progressed these wafers evolved into cookies, fruitcakes, and other goodies. At first these foods were shaped to represent some aspect of the Nativity, but in time they came to depict almost anything the decorator desired.

No one really seems to be able to explain the huge popularity of the Christmas tree, however along with Santa Claus it is now the most common secular item associated with Christmas in the United States. Trees were decorated as early as the Roman Saturnalia, but this custom did not become part of Christmas until the Middle Ages. The earliest record of a decorated tree is from an

English book printed in 1441, which describes a tree set up in the middle of a village and adorned with ivy. The Christmas tree enjoys incredible popularity to this day. One of the most anticipated events of the holiday season is the decorating of the family tree. In many German homes, each family member has a tree!

The Christmas tree had spread to Norway, Finland, Denmark, Sweden, and Austria by the 1800s. Fisherman in Scandinavia trimmed their trees with fish nets and flags. By the mid-nineteenth century, the Christmas tree had become extremely popular in America. The first church known in this country to display a tree was that of Reverend Henry Schwan in Cleveland, Ohio. The first people to popularize the Christmas tree in the White House were President and Mrs. Franklin Pierce. Most homes have some type of Christmas tree during the holidays, and trees can be found everywhere, from offices to churches to department stores.

Gifts

The union of Christmas and gift-giving was a gradual one. In ancient Rome, gifts were exchanged during Saturnalia and the New Year's celebration. The gifts were very simple—a few twigs from a sacred grove, food, and statues of gods. Many of the gifts included some type of vegetation in honor of the fertility goddess Strenia. As part of the northern European yule, fertility was celebrated with gifts made of wheat products such as alcohol and bread. Even though gift-giving was voluntary, as time went on the gifts became more elaborate and fewer edible gifts were given.

Like many of the old customs of the day, the gift exchange was difficult to get rid of as Christianity spread and gained official status. Early church leaders tried to ban the custom, but the people cherished it too deeply to let it go. So again church leaders sought a Christian basis for a pagan tradition. The justification was found in the Magi's act of bringing gifts to the baby Jesus. Further support came from the concept that Christ was a gift from God to the world, in turn bringing the gift of eternal life.

Even though Christmas celebrations were quite common, after Christianity established itself across Europe gift-giving on Christmas Day was not a component. The idea of exchanging gifts on the holiday remained an exception, so giving gifts was confined to New Year's, except in those countries with Spanish cultural influence, which saved gift-giving for January 6, the day marking the Magi's visit to Jesus.

The gift-giving tradition that we are familiar with comes primarily from Victorian England. After Christmas experienced a long period of decline, the Victorians brought a renewed warmth and spirit to the holiday. One important aspect to them was the act of helping the less fortunate in society. Giving gifts was a natural outgrowth of the friendliness and charity that filled so many hearts, and a great deal of thought and creativity went into each gift.

Even though Victorian gift-giving was filled with the spirit of Christmas, most of the actual exchanging was still done on New Year's Day. It wasn't until the late 1800s that the tradition finally was transferred to Christmas Day.

Greenery

Evergreens were revered by pagans for their ability to stay alive during the cold, dark winters. Often considered magical, greenery in various forms decorated the inside and outside of houses during the winter solstice festivals. At first, church officials tried to banish greenery, but later they decided it would better serve their purposes to translate the much loved custom into Christian terms. Evergreens thus came to symbolize Christ, who in His triumph over death gave the gift of eternal life to the world. The most common Christmas greens are holly, ivy, mistletoe, and of course the Christmas tree.

Holiday Feasts

Extravagant feasts played an important role in the winter solstice festivals of ages past. Besides a gathering place for people to have fun and exchange good will, these feasts displayed a certain faith in the prosperity of the coming year. Holiday feasting was at its peak in medieval England, where the king and his court were consistently trying to outdo each another with monstrous quantities of food and drink. Amazingly, the guests at these festivities preferred food to be presented looking as much like its animal of origin as possible, so the food was carefully crafted into shapes.

By Victorian times, roasted oxen, boar's head, and other wild animal meats had been replaced by goose, turkey, Yorkshire pudding, and plum pudding. Today, in the midst of the many traditional menu items, the main focus of these feasts is the gathering of family and friends.

Holly

Holly was thought to be magical in ancient times because of its shiny leaves and its ability to bear fruit in winter. Some people hung it over their beds to produce good dreams, while others believed it contained a syrup that cured coughs. Holly was a popular Saturnalia gift among Romans. They later brought holly to England, where it was considered sacred. Holly, along with ivy, became the subject of many Christmas songs in medieval times. Some songs gave the ivy and holly gender identities (ivy female, holly male), while other more religious songs and poems portrayed the holly berry as a symbol of Jesus Christ.

Midnight Mass

The Midnight Mass is the most popular Christmas Mass for Roman Catholics and is based on a legend claiming Christ was born at midnight. The tradition began in the early 400s. In Latin countries, the Midnight Mass is referred to as the "Mass of the Rooster," after the legend that says the only time a rooster ever crowed at midnight was the moment Christ was born. In Poland the Midnight Mass is called

Mass Pasterka, or "Mass of the Shepherds," in commemoration of the shepherds present in the accounts of the first Christmas.

Mistletoe

Many Christian churches still will not allow mistletoe—a parasitic plant that grows on oak and other non-evergreen trees—inside their buildings during the holiday season. Although other greenery was used in pagan festivals, mistletoe actually was worshipped. Both Romans and Druids considered the plant sacred—as a charm to ward off evil and as a healing plant. Because it grew out of roots, as if by magic, it was thought to be the link between heaven and earth. Mistletoe also was considered a symbol of peace. Fighting soldiers, who found themselves under some mistletoe, quickly put down their weapons and established a temporary truce. Ancient Britons hung mistletoe in their doorways to keep evil away. Those who safely entered the house were given a welcoming kiss.

Even though the tradition of kissing under the mistletoe lost popularity in many other countries, it has remained popular in the United States and England. Some people in France brew it as a cure for stomachaches, but most consider mistletoe nothing more than an excuse for kissing!

Nativity Scenes

The first Nativity scene was created in tenth-century Rome, at the church of Santa Maria Maggiore. The custom soon became popular with other churches. Each began constructing ornate mangers with silver, gold, jewels, and precious stones. Such extravagance was popular in high society, but it was obviously far removed from the original circumstance of Christ's birth, as well as being inaccessible to the poorer masses.

In 1224, St. Francis of Assisi sought to remedy these problems by creating a manger scene that was true to the biblical account of Christ's birth. Set up for the Italian village of Greccio, the scene, or *"crèche,"* was made of carved figures, hay, and live animals. The *crèche* captured for the average person more of the true spirit and story of Christ's birth. The popularity of St. Francis's *crèche* caught on quickly and eventually spread throughout the world. In Italy it is called a *presepio,* in the Czech Republic a *jeslicky,* in Costa Rica a *portal,* in Germany a *Krippe,* in Brazil a *pesebre,* and in Spain and Latin America a *naciemiento.*

Noël

Noël, the French word for Christmas, is derived from the Latin *(dies) natalis,* meaning "birthday." It was established in English through the popular Christmas carol "The First Noël." The word *"noël"* may also be traced to *nouvelles,* the French word for "the good news," because this is what the birth of Christ brought to the world. Others believe *noël* to be a corrupted rendering of the joyful claim that, with the Savior's coming, everything is "now well."

Ornaments

The earliest Christmas tree ornaments were edible—typically fruits and nuts, eventually becoming cakes, candy, and cookies. Paper decorations and flowers provided the non-edible beauty. The first "commercial" ornaments for Christmas were actually brightly colored, hollow containers that held goodies to eat. German glassblowers began manufacturing the first glass ornaments when the goodies got too heavy for the tree, however these and other wholly decorative elements would not be the most popular attraction for quite a number of years. Early on, trees were meant to display presents on Christmas morning before their owners claimed them. Small toys, candies, and other treats were hung on the branches, and children would awake and strip the tree of its goodies.

Poinsettia

The legend of the plant that is so strongly associated with Christmas came about many years ago in Mexico. There was a tradition of leaving gifts on the altar for Jesus on Christmas Eve. As the story is told, one night there was a young boy among a group of worshippers who did not have a present to give the Lord. Saddened by his inability to provide a gift, the boy knelt outside the church window and prayed. Right in the spot where he knelt sprung up a beautiful plant with vibrant red leaves. In Mexico the plant is called the "Flower of the Holy Night." Dr. Joel Roberts, the first American Ambassador to Mexico (1825–1829), was very impressed by this plant and is credited with bringing it to America.

Red and Green

No one really knows for sure why red and green are the dominant colors of Christmas. However, there have been many educated guesses. Green is the color of the evergreens, which were symbols of life to ancient Europeans. The red holly berry lives through the winter, symbolizing life in the face of death, and represents Christ.

Santa's Reindeer and Sleigh

The popularity of Santa and his reindeer is due largely to Clement C. Moore, who put the two together in his hugely successful poem "A Visit from St. Nicholas." However, Moore was not the first to put the two together. Before Moore's poem was published, a number of less successful books had portrayed Santa flying around in a sleigh pulled by one reindeer. This concept had long been popular in Russia, where "Father Frost" arrived in villages in a reindeer-drawn sleigh. There was also the legend of the Norse god Wodin, who was said to ride his horse Sleipner through the air to make sure people were behaving. In Holland, to this day, St. Nicholas is said to ride his horse Sleipner.

Today, Rudolph "the red-nosed reindeer" is without a doubt the most popular of Santa's herd of nine. He is also the youngest (or most recent arrival). The first eight reindeer were introduced by Moore in 1823. Rudolph did not arrive until 1939, in a story by Robert L. May. However, Rudolph owes much of his fame to Gene Autry, who recorded the popular song "Rudolph the Red-Nosed Reindeer." The song was released in 1949 and remains a holiday classic.

Stars

The star often found at the top of a Christmas tree or on a plate of Christmas cookies is patterned after the Star of Bethlehem. Its origin is strictly Christian. The nature of this star mentioned in the Bible remains something of a mystery, and has been a subject of scholarly debate for quite some time.

Stockings

The tradition of hanging stockings on Christmas Eve is thought to have come from Amsterdam. On St. Nicholas Eve, children leave their shoes out in hopes that the saint will fill them with goodies. The idea is thought to have come from St. Nicholas himself. As the legend has it, three daughters of marriageable age could not marry because they did not have a dowry. Nicholas heard of their plight and decided to help them. Wanting his actions to be a secret, Nicholas threw bags of gold coins down the girls' chimney in the middle of the night. The bags landed in their stockings, which they had hung up to dry.

Tinsel

A poor widow was determined to give her large family a memorable Christmas, but all she possessed was a simple tree. After spending many hours trimming her tree, she fell asleep exhausted. Spiders visited her home soon afterward. During the night they wove their webs all over the branches of her tree—

creating the original tinsel! As a reward for her goodness, Jesus is said to have miraculously changed the spider webs into silver threads which, reflecting light in magic brilliance, outshined anything ever seen before.

Wassail

Wassail surfaced as a popular Christmas drink in England during Victorian times. The name comes from the old toast: *waes hael* — "to your health." Wassail is made of eggs, curdled cream, nuts, spices, roasted apples, and fermented ale. In pagan times, wassail was believed to provide more than just good cheer. During agricultural festivals, groups of people would visit apple trees and douse them with wassail to ensure that the next harvest would be plentiful. This ritual also involved a great deal of noise-making to turn aside evil. The noise helped to foster a festive atmosphere. It was from this ritual that wassail's association with parties grew.

Xmas

The abbreviation of "Xmas" for Christmas is not sacrilegious. The first letter of the word "Christ" in Greek is "chi," or X, which is identical to our alphabet's X. Originally Xmas was an ecclesiastical abbreviation that was used in charts and tables. In the infant days of printing, font sizes were limited and type was set by hand, so ditto marks and abbreviations were used quite frequently. The church is actually the source of "Xmas," since it used the term when preparing to print Bibles.

Yule Log

The Teutons, Druids, and Celts burned massive logs in winter ceremonies in a pagan celebration of the sun. The selection of each season's yule log was very important and was surrounded by much fanfare and ceremony. The log not only started the celebration fires but was meant to last for the duration of the winter festival.

In the Christian adaptation, the log usually was cut on February 2—Candlemas Day—and then set outside to dry during the spring and summer. Oftentimes it was soaked in spices and decorated with greenery. Generally a piece from the previous year's log was used to light the new log. In Scandinavia, the piece from the previous year also represented good will from the god Thor. It was believed that Thor's lightning bolt would not strike already burned wood, thus their houses would be safe from lightning as long as they had a piece of the yule log.

With Christianity's emergence in Europe, the popularity of the yule log remained strong in England and Scandinavia. In order to help justify this pagan tradition, church officials gave it a new significance: The light from the log was said to have come from heaven when Christ was born. Traditionally the log was lit on Christmas Eve and left burning through the twelve days of Christmas.

In parts of France, the yule log was presented as the source of children's gifts. The log was brought into the house and covered with a cloth. Then the children whacked it with sticks and appealed to it to bring forth presents. When no presents came, the children were sent outside to confess their sins from that year. When they returned inside, the log was surrounded with gifts.

In the American South, plantation slaves always tried to choose the biggest possible yule log since the slaves had to be paid for any work they did while the log burned. The Industrial Revolution brought many changes that ultimately made the yule log impractical. Few people had the time, let alone the space, for the preparations it required. And the small fireplaces of the city could not accommodate such a massive activity. For most people, the yule log, like the boar's head, has become an emblem of the past.

The Santa Claus Tradition

Although his roots reach back into ancient times, Santa Claus has been popularized and redefined primarily through the media of the nineteenth and twentieth centuries. Two written accounts

—Clement C. Moore's 1822 "A Visit From St. Nicholas" and the *New York Sun's* famous response to a young girl named Virginia O'Hanlon's 1897 query about him—probably did the most to establish Santa as a popular figure in the Christmas celebration. Even though his most memorable characteristics are relatively recent, Santa Claus as we know him has evolved from a variety of sources over many years. The most notable of these is the life of St. Nicholas, an early Christian bishop in Asia Minor, present-day western Turkey. The accounts of St. Nicholas' life are a mixture of myth and fact. However there is no denying the impact this revered figure has had on the development of the Santa Claus tradition. St. Nicholas remains quite popular in Europe, where there are more churches named for him than for any other saint or apostle.

The basic facts surround a young man who became the bishop of Myra while still in his teens, earning the nickname "Boy Bishop." This bishop, Nicholas, through his generosity and courage is said to have touched the lives of many people and is credited with saving many from famine and despair. He founded an orphanage and was well known for his concern and love for children.

Stirring tales about Nicholas have made him very popular throughout Christendom. Consequently, in various European countries he is the patron saint of children, thieves, sailors, hoboes, pawnbrokers, and bankers. Nicholas is also the patron saint of Russia, Sicily, and Greece. Nicholas also was imprisoned by authorities of the Roman Empire during a time of religious persecution. Emperor Constantine, whose attitude towards Christianity was softening, finally reprieved Nicholas and others. Nicholas died on December 6, in A.D. 343, a day still celebrated as St. Nicholas Day in many European countries, and one that marks the beginning of the Christmas season.

Years after his death, his body was stolen from its crypt in Myra by sailors from Bari, Italy, who were seeking to protect his remains from Muslim invaders. The sailors brought the body to Bari and buried it in a basilica there. To this day, St. Nicholas Day is celebrated by the people of Bari on May 9, the date of the sailors' arrival. The theft of his body brought Nicholas the distinction of becoming the patron saint of thieves, and added to his already sizable legend.

Besides the evidence that Nicholas was a good man, there are many legends that surround his life. His birth is rumored to have been miraculous because his parents had been married more than thirty years and had given up hope of ever conceiving a child. Shortly after his birth, it is said that Nicholas was able to stand up in his crib, looking as if he were praying. The boy had no doubt about his vocation, as he began preparing to enter the monastery at a young age. Then came the gift of gold to the three young ladies, and his reputation as a generous, loving young man was born. As legend has it, the father of the three girls caught Nicholas in the act. Though Nicholas tried to swear the father to secrecy, the story spread rapidly through the town.

Nicholas became the bishop of Myra shortly after entering the monastery. The story is that the church in Myra had been having difficulty replacing the former bishop, and the people had become extremely discouraged as to how to solve the problem. Then one night a church official had a dream that the first man to enter the church for mass the next day should be the new bishop, and his name would be Nicholas. It just so happened that Nicholas had been traveling on a ship that encountered horrible weather. He prayed for safety, and when he arrived on dry land headed immediately for the church in Myra to give thanks. The rest is history.

St. Nicholas would also undergo another rough voyage on a ship many years later. As he was returning from a pilgrimage to the Holy Land, the ship that carried him ran into a terrible storm. Nicholas began praying for help. Witnesses on board the vessel claimed the sea calmed the moment Nicholas dropped to his knees. He became so important to sailors that Russian and Greek seaman always set sail with an icon of St. Nicholas, and he was declared the patron saint of sailors.

One of the most famous legends involves Nicholas stopping for rest at an inn during a journey. The innkeeper offered him some meat to eat, which had been made from the flesh of three little boys the innkeeper had killed. Although the stories vary concerning who the boys were, how they were killed, and whether they were stuck in pickle barrels or salt, the result remains the same: Nicholas figured out what the innkeeper was up to and brought the boys back to life. This act is commemorated in current St. Nicholas Day celebrations.

Due to Nicholas' status as the patron saint of sailors, his reputation spread to other lands. Dutch and Italian sailors introduced St. Nicholas to the West. By the Middle Ages, Nicholas was as popular in Europe as he was in his homeland. Vladimir of Russia discovered Nicholas in Constantinople in 1003 and brought his legend to his homeland, where Nicholas eventually became the patron saint.

Nowhere is the saint more celebrated than in Holland, where his name is Sinter Klaas. He wears breeches, like any respectable Dutchman, and has a long Dutch pipe and a broad-brimmed hat. The bearded Sinter Klaas rides a white horse and carries a basket of treats for good children—and birch rods for naughty ones. According to Dutch legend, Sinter Klaas spends the majority of the year in Spain with his servant Black Peter, a Moor, who keeps exacting records of the behavior of boys and girls. A few weeks before St. Nicholas Eve, Sinter Klaas packs up and heads for the Netherlands. He arrives by steamer on the last Saturday of November, dressed in full bishop regalia. The entire city turns out to greet him, and there is a ceremony featuring all the area officials. Nicholas spends the time before St. Nicholas Eve visiting hospitals, schools, and markets, giving small gifts to good kids while Black Peter switches the naughty ones (the dark side of the jolly old fellow we know today!). The largest presents are left to be opened on St. Nicholas Eve. Children are supposed to leave their shoes out at night, filled with hay for Sinter Klaas' horse, and are given gifts in return. These presents are unwrapped but cleverly hidden or disguised in some way. Each gift comes with a note that must be read out loud, and very often contains a line or two meant to embarrass the recipient. Some of these customs are carryovers from old Norse mythology and ritual. The god Wodin—whom the American St. Nicholas in the eighteenth century often resembled—was said to ride around on his horse checking up on little children.

Beginning in the sixteenth century, the Protestant Reformation led many places in Europe to reject the cult of saints and anything associated with them. The legend of St. Nicholas might have died except for his popularity. Subsequently, most countries changed his name slightly while leaving his background intact. To the French he became *Pere Noël*; to the English he became Father Christmas. Though many people incorrectly assign the German name for the Christ child—*Christkindl*, or Kris Kringle—the accurate German equivalent is *Weihnachtsmann* or "Christmas man."

Gift-givers differing from St. Nicholas only in name and a few details can be found in other places across Europe. Russia's *Nikolai Chudovorits* evolved into Father Frost, who lives beyond the Arctic Circle. He comes to Russia on New Year's Day in a sleigh drawn by reindeer, accompanied by his daughter the Snow Maiden, to place presents under trees. The Scandinavian gift-givers are much more playful and mischievous. The Danish *Julenisse*, Norwegian *Julebukk* or *Julesvenn*, and the Swedish *Jultomten* all visit on St. Nicholas Eve. Children leave treats out for them, in an effort to persuade them to do the same, as well as to dissuade them from trickery.

The legend of St. Nicholas was incorporated into the winter solstice festivals which later became part of the Christmas celebration. For a long time St. Nicholas day began the Christmas season, and eventually, because of the closeness in time, many cultures merged St. Nicholas Day and Christmas. In France and Germany, for example, most of the activities surrounding St.

Nicholas' Eve have been transferred to Christmas Eve. The majority of European countries, however, still keep the two separate. Goodies and gifts are still given on both days.

St. Nicholas came to America by way of the Dutch in the 1600s. Sinter Claes, as the name was rendered, was an important figure to the Dutch settlers. They named their first church in the New World the St. Nicholas Collegiate Church, even though it was Protestant. In the Dutch settlement of New Amsterdam—later named New York City—St. Nicholas Day and Christmas were celebrated in a grand fashion unknown to much of Colonial America. Because of the strict Puritan background of many of the New World settlers, any celebration of saints or Christmas was out of the question.

Amazingly, Christmas was illegal in New England until 1681, and then it was observed in a strict religious sense. Essentially it was not celebrated in any meaningful way before the American Revolution. In the years after the war, Christmas slowly began to win acceptance as a cause for celebration in various regions of the United States, but only at the dawn of the nineteenth century would any meaningful references to the one we call Santa Claus appear. This change in national attitude can be traced primarily to two factors: the influx of German immigrants to the country, and the intermarriage of the Pennsylvania Dutch with other settlers.

Some of the earliest American literary treatments of the St. Nicholas legend came at the turn of the century from Washington Irving's satires of New Amsterdam society. The evolution from St. Nicholas to today's American Santa Claus did not begin in earnest until twenty or thirty years later. In 1822, Clement C. Moore's hugely influential poem "A Visit from St. Nicholas" was published anonymously. Within a few years it had become widely popular, and in 1837, in response to enthusiastic public support, Moore finally acknowledged authorship. Although his lines were most influential in creating an image of the modern-day Santa Claus, nowhere does that name appear in the poem.

Moore wrote the verses for his own children, reciting it for his family for the first time on Christmas Eve. He got the plumpness for Santa from a rotund gardener who worked for him, but the description of a small, round man, with twinkling eyes and a small beard, sounds more like an elf than our current depictions:

> He was dressed all in fur from his head to his foot, And his clothes were all tarnished with ashes and soot; A bundle of toys he had flung on his back, And he looked like a peddler just opening his pack. His eyes, how they twinkled! His dimples, how merry! His cheeks were like roses, his nose like a cherry; His droll little mouth was drawn up like a bow, And the beard on his chin was as white as snow. The stump of his pipe he held tight in his teeth, And the smoke it encircled his head like a wreath. He had a broad face and a little round belly that shook, when he laughed, like a bowl full of jelly.[2]

Moore's portrayal of St. Nicholas as a friend to children and a generous gift-giver was an outgrowth of the legends surrounding St. Nicholas. The poem's emphasis on snowy winter weather could be due to earlier traditions linking Nicholas with winter cold, or simply to the fact that Moore himself enjoyed a white Christmas season the winter he wrote the poem. Moore was not the first to connect reindeer to St. Nicholas, however he was the first to set the total at eight. He also created the names we now associate with those animals:

> Now Dasher, now Dancer, now Prancer and Vixen,
> On Comet, on Cupid, on Donner and Blitzen!

In 1842, a popular children's book featured illustrations of a stout, bearded, gift-giving character referred to as Kris Kringle. Although uniform pictures of this figure would not surface for another twenty years, the drawings in the book were in fact the first modern representations of the St. Nicholas we envision today. The name by which we commonly know him would not gain currency until the middle of the century, when pronunciation of Sinter Claes somehow changed to Santa Claus.

Although Moore's poem had greater influence on our vision of Santa, the *New York Sun's* editorial response to young Virginia O'Hanlon's inquiry about his existence has probably had the greatest effect on the way we *think* about him. The piece, which first ran in 1897, has resurfaced every holiday season thereafter, capturing for kids and adults the innocence and trust of the Santa Claus tradition. The *Sun* article also supplied the nation with the now-famous catch-phrase, "Yes, Virginia, there is a Santa Claus." This was the turning point that finally gave the United States a single perception of the bearded one to which publishers and marketers alike could appeal. The final touches of a smiling, chubby figure were formalized in the 1920s by artist Haddon Sundblom in a series of Coca-Cola ads. Sundblom's Santa wore a red gown with white trim, had red cheeks, and radiated a rotund good cheer. As no surprise, Santa also liked Coke. The ad campaign ran for thirty-five years and was even revived recently.

What's a Christian to Do With Santa?

There will come a time in the life of every parent when he or she will have to decide what to do with Santa Claus. What is the right thing to do with this jolly fellow in a red suit and a reindeer-powered sleigh? Must we choose between Jesus or Santa, or are there other options?

We can choose to simply not participate in anything at all associated with Santa Claus. This is certainly a valid option, but it does present a problem that will need to be dealt with when your children are young. Santa Claus is a big part of the Christmas season in our culture, and kids will want to know why they can't do what their relatives and friends at school and in the neighborhood are doing with Santa. This is definitely not an insurmountable problem, but it is one that you'll have to be prepared to resolve.

I think it is possible to allow our children to have the Santa Claus tradition as part of their holiday celebration and still not miss out on the real reason for the season. For one thing, I think it's extremely difficult to make the connection between modern-day Santa Claus and ancient pagan rituals. It seems doubtful enough that St. Nicholas would even recognize himself in Santa if the two were to meet face to face. And while there is no doubt the spirit found in Clement C. Moore's poem has been greatly over-shadowed by the retail madness of our day, if we return to Moore's emphasis on being a friend to children and a generous gift-giver, it is a tradition worth considering as part of our holiday season.

There are many worthwhile activities that are part of our culture for which we have no biblical example—birthday cakes and Mother's Day roses come to mind. Some things have become an integral part of our culture, even if we don't know everything about their histories. The whole concept of gift-giving and receiving obviously has the ultimate example in the precious gift God gave to the world that very first Christmas. Our main concern must be keeping Christ as the central focus of Christmas and not letting any holiday traditions—including Santa Claus—diminish the true reason for the season. If you are wise in how you incorporate the Santa tradition, it can be fun for you and your children and can provide a great opportunity for family discussion about Christmas as the birthday of Jesus.

I was being interviewed on a radio talk show regarding my book, *Halloween: What's a Christian to Do?*, when a woman called the show and exclaimed, "I don't have anything to do with something unless it's in the Bible." I chuckled before responding, "Do you drive a car? Do you use a telephone or have electricity in your home? Because none of these are mentioned in the Bible." I appreciated her desire to remain biblically focused, but wanted her to see the flaw in her reasoning. There is an excellent principle found in 1 Corinthians 10:31 to help parents struggling with the issue of Santa: "So whether you eat or drink or whatever you do, do it all for the glory of God."

We must always ask ourselves, "Is this glorifying God?"

We can keep our celebration of Christmas creative, fun, and joyful. But most of all, let's glorify God in the process. After all, where would we be without His "indescribable gift"?

3

Christmas
Around the World

Have you ever wondered what happens in Australia where Christmas falls in the middle of summer vacation? Or what's for Christmas dinner in Sweden? And how do people celebrate the holiday in Italy? There are not many people who are aware of the various ways Christmas is observed around the world. From the tiniest villages to the largest city, from the jungles of Africa to the high-rises of Hong Kong, there are Christmas celebrations around the world.

Christmas in China

Christians in China celebrate by lighting their houses with beautiful paper lanterns and decorating their Christmas trees—which they call "Trees of Light"—with paper flowers, chains, and lanterns. Children hang up muslin stockings and wait for a visit from Santa Claus, whom they call *Dun Che Lao Ren,* which means "Old Man Christmas."

Because the vast majority of Chinese people are not Christians, the main winter festival in China is the Chinese New Year, which takes place toward the end of January. Officially called the "Spring Festival," it is a time when children eat luscious meals, receive new clothing and toys, and enjoy fireworks displays. An important aspect of the New Year celebration is the worship of ancestors.

Pictures and portraits of forebears are brought out and hung in the main room of the home.

Christmas in India

In India, Christians decorate banana or mango trees at Christmastime. They also decorate their houses with mango leaves and, in some parts of India, use small clay oil-burning lamps as Christmas decorations. These are placed on the edges of flat roofs and on the tops of walls. For Christmas Eve services, churches are decorated with poinsettias and lit with candles.

Christmas in Japan

Christian missionaries introduced Christmas to Japan. For many years, the only people who celebrated the holiday were those who had been converted to the Christian faith. However, now the Christmas season in Japan is full of meaning and is almost universally observed. The concept of exchanging gifts strongly appeals to the Japanese people. Stores have commercialized Christmas, just as our shops in the West have, and several weeks before December 25 stores are exploding with Christmas decorations.

Many Western traditions have been adopted by the Japanese. In addition to exchanging gifts, they also eat turkey on Christmas Day, houses are decorated with evergreens and mistletoe, and in some places there are even community Christmas trees. There is a god or a priest in Japan, known as *Hoteiosho,* who closely resembles our Santa Claus. He is thought to have eyes in the back of his head and is always portrayed as a kind old man carrying a huge pack. Obviously, it is important for children to be good when this all-seeing gentleman is around.

The story of the Christ child born in a manger is fascinating to the little girls of Japan, for they love anything to do with babies. Through the Nativity scene they become familiar for the first time with a cradle, since Japanese babies never sleep in them.

Christmas in Korea

Christians in Korea celebrate Christmas with traditional religious services. Schoolchildren put on pageants, and there is a great deal of effort put into helping the needy. For the actual Christmas service, children and adults stay awake in the church on Christmas Eve. Around 2 a.m., they go out into the neighborhood singing and are often invited into homes for a treat. Religious services are held in the morning, and there is much caroling as people make their way to church.

Christmas in Africa

Although Christmas has been a tradition in Ethiopia for a long time, observance in most other African countries is limited to areas with established missions. Christmas in these areas is observed simply, in a way that many feel reflects the true meaning of the holiday. During Christmastime, the efforts of all are concentrated on helping those in need and on the spiritual aspects of the holiday. For the most part, there are no Santas or trees and there is little gift-giving, except to the poor. In some areas, lucky children receive sugar, grains, or fruit.

In Algiers, streets are colorfully decorated and there are a number of Catholic churches that celebrate Midnight Mass. The Christian church in Ethiopia is the Coptic church. Believers there abide by an ancient calendar, which places Christmas on January 7. In Liberia mission schools give gifts and decorate palm trees.

In Ghana things stray from the norm for the rest of the continent. Here Christmas evergreen or palm trees are seen, though only in churches. Also, there is a Father Christmas who comes out of the jungle with gifts. Children have school pageants, and early on Christmas morning a group enacts the story of the shepherds and angels heralding Christ's birth. They travel the streets and sing songs, and often are rewarded with gifts.

It's safe to say that in most African countries Christmas could be ignored entirely without changing the cultural landscape. The one exception is the nation of South Africa. Christmas there falls in the middle of summer vacation, so the festivities are adapted to the warmer weather. In the European sections of the country, streets are lit and shops are decorated, and Father Christmas puts gifts in the children's stockings. After church on Christmas Day, the Christmas feast is eaten outside. The non-European sections have feasts, parades, and carnivals.

Christmas in Australia

As in South Africa, Christmas falls during summer vacation in Australia. Because of the climate, flowers are the most important Christmas decoration—especially the Christmas Bush and the Christmas Bell. Santa and Father Christmas exist side by side, and gifts are exchanged on Christmas morning before church. Usually the afternoon is spent at the beach or engaging in sports.

"Down under" is also the home of "Carols by Candlelight," a tradition started by radio announcer Norman Banks in 1937. Banks saw a woman listening to carols by candlelight and decided to do something to relieve the isolation and loneliness some people feel during the holidays. He announced a community sing for anyone who wanted to join in. Over the years, the concept has grown in popularity and the pre-recorded program is now broadcast around the world.

Christmas in England

Many of our contemporary ideals in America about the way Christmas ought to be celebrated come from the English Victorian Christmas, like that described in Charles Dickens' A Christmas Carol. The gifts, the feast, the caroling, and the wishing of good cheer to all—these ingredients came together to create that unique Christmas atmosphere.

As we noted earlier, for many years in England, a roasted boar's head has been associated with holiday feasting, having been borrowed from an old Norse ritual. However, the observance of the Feast of St. Stephen on December 26 is part of the holiday season unique to Great Britain. It is on this day that the alms box at every English church is opened and the contents are distributed to the poor. This is also the day that servants in earlier times got the day off to celebrate with their families, and it became customary for working people to break open their tip boxes and retrieve the coins inside—thus the more common name, "Boxing Day." Boxing Day began in the mid-nineteenth century when the custom of tipping by rich people to those in service positions was expanded to include giving to everyone who had less money than the giver did. The streets soon became crowded with con men and others aggressively soliciting tips. To contain the growing nuisance, Boxing Day was designated as the one day for giving to the less fortunate.

Christmas in Ireland

In Ireland, Christmas is more religious and less festive than in other parts of Europe. Lit candles are left in the windows on Christmas Eve to light the way for the Holy Family, but there are seldom many other decorations. The door to the home is left open on Christmas Eve so that the Holy Family may partake of the bread and milk left out on the table. Father Christmas is the gift-giver here, and for a special treat three puddings are made: one for Christmas, one for New Year's, and one for the Twelfth Night, also called the Epiphany.

In Ireland, St. Stephen's Day is celebrated in a different way, but is somewhat similar to Boxing Day in that it also has to do with the solicitation of money. Young men in lavish costumes, sometimes with masks, noisily parade through the streets in the Wren Boy's Procession. They carry a long pole, on top of which is attached a holly bush. Supposedly the bush contains a captured wren, for whose sake the young men beg for money.

Christmas in Scotland

In Scotland, Christmas is celebrated rather somberly, merriment being reserved for New Year's Eve, called *Hogmanay*. This word is apparently derived from a kind of oat cake that was traditionally served to children on New Year's Eve. The Scots believe that the first person to set foot in a house in a New Year will profoundly affect the fortunes of the residents. Most of the time, strangers are thought to bring good luck, but whether it's better to have a fair-haired or dark-haired stranger set foot in the house depends on the area. This tradition is widely known as "first footing."

Christmas in Wales

Caroling is very popular in Wales, where it is called *eisteddfoddle* and is often accompanied by a harp. In some rural areas a villager is chosen to be the *Mari Ilwyd*. This person travels around town draped in white and carrying a horse's skull on a long pole. Anyone who gets "bitten" by the horse's jaws must then pay a fine.

Christmas in Canada

Because Canada is made up of a variety of ethnic groups, most celebrate Christmas in accordance with their own traditions. Vancouver, on the western end of Canada, is illuminated with lights —especially in the harbor area—and trees are lit in homes. In Montreal, masses are celebrated in the many magnificent cathedrals. In Nova Scotia, old carols are sung in church and at home. In Newfoundland, the residents' fishing skills are put to work for the church. During Christmas week the daily catch is given to the church so that it can be sold to raise money for the work of the church.

Christmas in Belgium

St. Nicholas arrives in Belgium on December 4 to take a look around and gauge children's behavior. On December 6 he delivers special treats to good children and gives switches to bad ones. The children leave their shoes outside, along with water and hay for his horse, as an added measure of goodness.

Flanders is an area of the country that is famous for its Nativity plays, performed with great attention to tradition. Three men who are chosen for their lifestyle and character during the year dress as Magi and walk through the town. They sing songs at each house and are rewarded with snacks. On Christmas Eve in Belgium, there are extensive processions everywhere. Each procession winds through town, picking up members as it flows, until it reaches the church for Midnight Mass.

Christmas in France

For the French, the winter holiday known as *Noël* is especially important to children. The season is a time to bask in the innocence and wonder of youth, while remembering the Holy Child who started it all. *Noël,* from an expression meaning "day of birth," begins for most French on December 6, St. Nicholas' Day. That day is celebrated most heartily in the provinces, especially in Lorraine, as it is believed that the Virgin Mary gave Lorraine to Nicholas as a gift. He is the patron saint not only of Lorraine but of children as well. Little ones leave out their shoes in hopes that St. Nicholas will leave gifts of candy and nuts during his night visit. The signs of the season begin to appear rapidly after St. Nicholas' Day. Homes, streets, shopping malls, cafés, and shops are adorned with lights, colorful decorations, and the image of *Pere Noël.*

At Christmastime, in nearly every French home is displayed a *crèche,* or Nativity scene. This serves as the focus for the Christmas celebration. The *crèche* is often decorated with little clay figures called *santons,* or "little saints." The use of these little figures, which are made by craftsmen throughout the year in the south of France, has evolved into quite an extensive tradition. Besides the usual Holy Family, shepherds, and Magi, the craftsmen produce figures to represent local dignitaries and characters. The workmanship in creating the beautifully colored santons is incredible, and the molds have been passed on from generation to generation since the seventeenth century. The figures are sold at annual Christmas fairs throughout December in Marseille and Aix.

Flowers are another staple decoration in the French home during the holiday season. Lush arrangements of roses, gladioli, carnations, and snapdragons often are found on the table or next to the fireplace. There are also poinsettias, hyacinths, azaleas, and Christmas begonias.

The Christmas tree never has been very popular in France. Most who take trees home pot them so they will last longer and may be planted later. Even though the popularity of the yule log has faded, the French still make a traditional yule log-shaped cake called the *buche de Nol,* or "Christmas Log." The cake, along with other food in great abundance, is served at the grand feast of the holiday season, which is called *le reveillon* ("the awakening"). *Le reveillon* is a late supper served after Midnight Mass on Christmas Eve and may have as many as fifteen courses. The menu for the meal varies depending upon the regional culinary tradition, but could include soups, fruits, salads, meats, fish, chicken, cheese breads, nuts, pastry, candy, and wine. In Alsace, goose is the main course, in Burgundy it's turkey with chestnuts, and Parisians feast on oysters.

The arrival of Christmas Eve sees the infant Jesus finally taking his place in the family *crèche* after a small family ceremony. Little children are then put to bed, left to hope that the gifts they asked for will be left by *Pere Noël.* He travels the countryside with his stern disciplinarian partner *Pre Fouettard.*

Pere Noël is reminded by *Pre Fouettard* of just how well each child has behaved during the past year. In some parts of France, *Pere Noël* brings small gifts on St. Nicholas Eve (December 6) and returns for another visit again on Christmas Eve. In other places it is *le petit Jesus* who brings gifts. In general, adults wait until New Year's Day to exchange gifts.

Christmas in Germany

In no other country is Christmas more universally and elaborately celebrated than in Germany, and many of our most popular holiday traditions have their roots there. The Christmas season officially begins four Sundays before Christmas Day with the beginning of Advent. German Lutherans originated the tradition of the Advent wreath, a circle of greenery in which four candles are set. One candle is lit on the first Sunday of Advent, two are lit the second Sunday, and so on until the fourth Sunday. Then a large white candle, in the center, is lit on Christmas Day. Also originating in Germany is the Advent calendar—an elaborate calendar with small windows, used to count down the days until Christmas.

The widespread popularity of the Christmas tree comes from Germany. During the Middle Ages, Germans would put on a mystery play each December 24, known as the Feast of Adam and Eve. The plays always featured a decorated evergreen tree representing the Tree of the Knowledge of Good and Evil, from which Adam and Eve ate. They were banished from the Garden of Eden as a result. Over the course of many years the plays and associated festivities drifted from their religious origins, and the church quit sponsoring them. However, people continued to set up and decorate trees in their homes each year at Christmastime. Glassmakers in Thuringia discovered how to make blown glass balls and bells in 1880, and these became the decorations used to trim Christmas trees all over the world.

Enchanting markets, with colorfully decorated booths and stalls, are set up for weeks before Christmas in many German cities. The Christmas market in Nuremberg is the most famous of these. It has a rich history of more than 400 years and is attended by people from many different countries. The festival lasts for three weeks, from early December until Christmas, and only items related to Christmas are offered for sale. Visitors can enjoy a magnificent view from the main market square of the famous *Schner Brunnen* ("beautiful fountain") and the 600-year-old *Frauenkirche* ("Our Lady's Church"). In Germany, as in many European nations, the high point of the Christmas season is Midnight Mass on Christmas Eve. The service is celebrated by both Catholics and Protestants.

Traditionally, St. Nicholas has brought gifts to German children on the eve of his feast day, December 6. He travels with a sometimes frightening, dark-faced companion known by a variety of names, including *Krampus, Pelzebock, Pelznickel, Hans Muff, Bartel,* or *Gumphinkel*. Most commonly, St. Nicholas's companion is called *Knecht Ruprecht* and carries a bundle of switches.

After the Reformation, church authorities frowned upon the idea of having a character representing the bishop distributing gifts. This resulted in St. Nick's present-day incarnation. Santa Claus was born, complete with red suit, long white beard, and sleigh. In various regions of Germany, Santa Claus is known by different names, including *Klaasbuur, Burklaas, Sunnercia, Rauklas,* and *Bullerklaas*. The Santa figure remains more connected with his pagan past in eastern Germany and is known as Ash Man, Rider, or Shaggy Goat. Today he is increasingly known throughout Germany as Father Christmas, and he now appears on Christmas Eve, not on St. Nicholas Eve.

Christmas in Greece

St. Nicholas is important in Greece because he is the patron saint of sailors. According to Greek legend, his beard drips with sea water, his face is covered with perspiration, and his clothes are drenched with brine because he has been working hard against the waves to reach sinking ships and rescue them from the angry sea. Today a Greek ship will not leave port without some kind of St. Nicholas icon on board.

In the roster of important holidays Christmas ranks second to Easter to members of the Eastern Orthodox Church, and there are a number of particular customs associated with Christmas that are uniquely Greek. On Christmas Eve, children travel from house to house in the villages singing *kalanda* (the equivalent of carols) and offering good wishes. Many times the songs are accompanied by little clay drums and small metal triangles. Neighbors frequently reward the children with dried fruits and sweets.

Christmas trees are not commonly used. Instead, in almost every home the main symbol of the holiday season is a shallow wooden bowl with a piece of wire suspended across the rim. From the wire hangs a sprig of basil, wrapped around a wooden cross. To keep the basil fresh, a small amount of water is kept in the bottom of the bowl. Once per day, a family member—usually the mother—dips the cross and basil into some holy water and uses it to sprinkle water into each room of the house. People in Greece believe this ritual keeps away the *Killantzaroi*—mischievous goblins who slip down people's chimneys during the twelve days of Christmas and extinguish fires, braid horses' tails, and make milk go sour. To further help repel the undesirable goblins, a fire is kept burning in the hearth twenty-four hours a day from December 25 to January 6.

The Christmas feast is regarded with great anticipation by children and adults alike. Pigs are slaughtered, and on almost every table are loaves of *Christopsomo,* or "Christ Bread." This bread is made in large, sweet loaves of different shapes, and the crusts are engraved and decorated in some way that reflects the family's profession. Gifts are exchanged on St. Basil's Day (January 1). The ritual of "renewal of waters" also takes place this day, in which all water jugs are emptied and refilled with new "St. Basil's Water."

Christmas in Italy

The popularity of the Nativity scene—one of the most loved and enduring symbols of Christmas—originated in Italy. Saint Francis of Assisi asked a man named Giovanni Velita, from the small village of Greccio, to create a manger scene and his handiwork inspired reverence and awe in all who saw it. The creation of the *pastori* (figures) developed into an entire genre of folk art.

Throughout the season, houses, stores, and streets are decorated in traditional ways, and there is much music and singing. The *ceppo* is an Italian version of the Christmas tree. Made of wood, the *ceppo* has the appearance of a ladder, with shelves linking two sides. The miniature manger's other shelves contain gifts and decorations.

On Christmas Eve in Rome, cannons are fired from Castel St. Angelo to announce the beginning of the holiday season. A strict twenty-four-hour fast ends on Christmas Eve with an elaborate feast, and small presents are drawn from the "Urn of Fate." This unique feature is a bowl filled with both presents and empty boxes. Each person picks to see whether he or she is "fated" to receive a gift—although no one ever really goes away empty-handed. However, the main exchange of gifts takes place on January 6, called the Feast of the Epiphany. This celebration is in remembrance of the Magi's visit to the Christ child. Young children anxiously await a visit from *La Befana*, who brings gifts for those who have been good and punishes those who have been bad. According to tradition, the three wise men stopped during their journey and asked an old woman for shelter and food. She refused them, and they continued on their way. Within a few hours, the old woman had a change of heart, but the Magi were long gone. *La Befana*, which means Epiphany, is said to still be wandering the earth in search of the Christ child. She can be depicted in a variety of ways, including as a fairy queen, a crone, or a witch.

Christmas in Spain

Christmas is a very religious holiday in Spain. The Christmas season officially begins December 8 with the Feast of the Immaculate Conception. It is celebrated each year in front of the grand Gothic Cathedral in Seville with a ceremony called *los Seises* — "the Dance of Six." Interestingly, the intricate dance ritual is now performed by ten elaborately costumed boys instead of just six. It is said to be quite moving to watch the series of precise movements and gestures.

Christmas Eve is known as *Nochebuena*, or "the Good Night." It's a great time for families to gather together to feast and celebrate around the Nativity scenes that are present in almost every home. A favorite traditional Christmas treat is *turron,* an almond-like candy. December 28 in Spain is the Feast of the Holy Innocents. Young boys in each village or town light bonfires and one of them acts as mayor. The "acting mayor" orders townspeople to perform certain civic chores like sweeping the streets. If someone refuses to comply, it results in a fine that is used to help pay for the celebration.

As is tradition in many European countries, children in Spain receive gifts on the Feast of the Epiphany. The Magi are particularly revered in Spain, and it is believed that every year at this time they travel throughout the countryside reenacting their journey to Bethlehem. Children follow the tradition of leaving their shoes on the windowsills and filling them with straw and carrots to feed the horses of the Wise Men. The children's favorite is Balthazar, who rides a donkey and who supposedly leaves the candy.

Christmas in Portugal

The celebration of Christmas in Portugal is very similar to what takes place in Spain, but the Portuguese enjoy an additional feast called *Consoada* in the early morning hours of Christmas Day. Extra places are set at the table for *alminhas a penar* — the souls of the dead. In some houses they leave crumbs on the hearth for these souls, a tradition that derives from the ancient practice of entrusting seeds to the dead in hopes that they will provide a bountiful harvest.

Christmas in The Netherlands

In the Netherlands St. Nicholas is known as *Sinter Klaas.* Dutch children are taught that he sails from Spain on his feast day, December 6. The night before, they leave their shoes out filled with sugar and hay for his horse. In the morning they awake to find their shoes filled with small gifts.

On occasion, *Sinter Klaas* appears in person in the children's homes, bearing an incredible resemblance to the kids' uncle or father. *Sinter Klaas* then questions the children about their behavior during the past year. Many years ago he carried a birch rod with which to punish previous poor behavior, but these days he is known to be much kinder.

There is a special Advent service held by people who live in Twente or east Holland. During the ceremony unique horns are blown to chase away evil spirits and to declare the birth of Christ. These horns are made by hand out of one-year-old saplings and are three to four feet long. When they are blown over wells, they have a deep sound, very similar to that of a foghorn.

Christmas in Denmark

In Denmark, the Christmas feast is celebrated at midnight on Christmas Eve. Everyone's favorite part of the meal is dessert, when a special rice pudding is served in which is hidden a single almond. Whoever finds the almond will have good luck for the coming year.

Julemanden is known as the jolly bringer of gifts, and arrives with a sack over his back in a sleigh drawn by reindeer. He is assisted with his Christmas chores by elves called *Juulnisse,* who are said to live in attics. On Christmas Eve children leave out saucers of rice pudding or milk for them and are delighted to find the food gone on Christmas morning.

Christmas in Norway

Like other Scandinavian countries, Norway has its own gift-bearing elf. Known as *Julebukk,* or "Christmas Buck," he appears as a goatlike creature. *Julebukk* dates back to Viking times when pagans worshipped Thor and his goat. During celebrations a person dressed in a goatskin and carrying a goat head would "crash" the party. Over the course of the evening, this person would "die" and return to life. Then during the early part of the Christian era, the goat began to take the form of the devil and would appear during wild party times. By the end of the Middle

Ages, the game was forbidden by the state and the church. In more recent times the goat has emerged in the tamer form of *Julebukk*.

Christmas in Sweden

A thousand years ago, King Canute declared that Christmas would last a month, from December 13 (The Feast of St. Lucia) until January 13, or *Tjugondag Knut* (St. Canute's Day). No one is really quite sure why Lucia, a fourth-century Sicilian saint, came to be so revered in Sweden. Some believe missionaries brought stories of her life that entranced the Swedish people, while others say she once visited the country. Her story was birthed in the early days of Christian persecution, when Lucia carried food to Christians hiding in dark underground tunnels. To light the way she wore a wreath of candles on her head. Ultimately Lucia was arrested and martyred.

On the day of the Feast of St. Lucia, the eldest daughter in each family dresses in a white gown with a red sash and wears an evergreen wreath with seven lighted candles on her head. She carefully carries buns and coffee to each family member in their room. Many schools, businesses, and communities sponsor Lucia processions in which carols are sung and everyone thanks the "Queen of Light" for bringing hope during the darkest time of the year.

On Christmas Eve, a certain Christmas gnome—known as the *tomte*—emerges from his home under the floor of the house or barn. He carries a big sack over his shoulder and leaves gifts for everyone.

Yuletide, or the winter solstice, has traditionally been a time of extreme importance in Sweden and the rest of Scandinavia. This was considered a time when fortunes for the coming year were determined and when the dead were thought to walk the earth. For a long time it was considered dangerous to sleep alone on Christmas Eve. Thus the extended family, master and servant alike, would sleep together on a freshly spread bed of straw.

Christmas in Czechoslovakia

Hundreds of years ago, the western half of Czechoslovakia was known as Bohemia. This was the tenth-century home of Good King Wenceslas, the main character in the popular English Christmas carol. Tradition says that it was English troops, fighting in Bohemia hundreds of years later, who brought the song home with them. St. Nicholas is called *Svaty Mikalas* and is thought to have climbed down from heaven to earth on a golden rope, along with his companions: an angel and a whip-carrying devil.

An ancient holiday tradition shared by Czechoslovakia and Poland involves cutting a branch from a cherry tree and putting it in water to bloom. If the bloom opens in time for Christmas, it is considered good luck and a sign that winter may be short. This hope of an early spring helps keep spirits up during the dark of winter.

Christmas in Poland

An elaborate tradition called *Wigilia* is celebrated in Poland. Starting on Christmas Eve, a strict 24-hour fast is observed which ends with a huge Christmas feast. In honor of the Star of Bethlehem, the meal cannot begin until the first star of the evening appears. Though Christmas in Poland is officially known as *Bozz Narodzenie,* it is most commonly referred to as *Gwiazdka,* which means "little star." Once the star appears, a special rice wafer, called *oplatek,* blessed by the parish priest, is broken into pieces and shared by all the members of the family. At last the meal can begin. The feast consists of twelve courses—one for each Apostle. The table is always set with one extra seat in case a stranger or the Holy Spirit should appear to share the meal.

Christmas in Romania

The Christmas tradition in Romania is for children to travel, in a group, from house to house singing carols and reciting poetry and legends. The leader carries a large wooden star called a *steaua,* which is covered with shiny paper and decorated with colored ribbon and bells. A picture of the Holy Family is pasted to the star's center, and the entire creation is attached to a broomstick or strong pole.

Christmas in Russia

St. Nicholas is especially popular in Russia. Legend has it that the eleventh-century Prince Vladimir traveled to Constantinople to be baptized. He returned with stories of miracles performed by St. Nicholas of Myra. Since that time many Eastern Orthodox Churches have been named for the saint, and to this day Nicholas is one of the most popular names for Russian boys. The feast of St. Nicholas, on December 6, was observed for many centuries. After the Russian Revolution, the celebration of the feast was suppressed and St. Nicholas was transformed into Grandfather Frost.

Other religious traditions were also suppressed. Prior to the revolution, a figure called *Babouschka* would bring gifts for the children. Like Italy's *La Befana*, the story is that *Babouschka* failed to give food and shelter to the three wise men during their journey to visit the Christ child. According to legend, she still roams the countryside visiting the homes of children during the Christmas season and searching for the Lord. *Babouschka* never completely disappeared, and now in the post-communist era has returned openly. The Communist regime also banned Christmas trees, but people continued to trim their "New Year's" trees.

Many Russian Christians belong to the Eastern Orthodox Church, and it is customary to fast until after the first church service on Christmas Eve. The Christmas Eve dinner is meatless, but the most important ingredient is a special porridge called *kutya*. It's made of wheat berries or other grains, which symbolize immortality and hope. It also includes honey and poppy seeds, which are said to ensure happiness, success, and peace. The *kutya* is eaten from a common dish to symbolize unity. A special ceremony to bless the home is also frequently observed. A priest visits the home accompanied by boys carrying vessels of holy water. A little water is then sprinkled into each room.

Christmas in Mexico

Several weeks before Christmas, elaborately decorated market stalls called *puestos* are set up in the plazas of every town and city. Many people travel for days from remote areas to get to these markets. The *puestos* offer foods like cheese, bananas, nuts, and cookies, crafts of every conceivable kind, and flowers like poinsettias and orchids. The poinsettia is native to Mexico and is thought to have been first used in connection with Christmas in the seventeenth century when Mexican Franciscans included flowers in their Christmas celebration.

Mexico's main Christmas celebration is called *las posadas,* which refers to processions reenacting Joseph and Mary's search for a place to stay in Bethlehem. These processions begin nine days before Christmas because the original journey from Nazareth to Bethlehem took nine days. Family members and friends divide themselves into two groups: innkeepers and pilgrims. The pilgrims travel from house to house asking for shelter and are refused at each stop until they finally reach the house where the altar and Nativity scene have been set up. Here the Pilgrims are welcomed with great rejoicing; then a traditional prayer is spoken and the party begins. Food and drink are served, and the children take turns trying to break the *piñata.*

Christmas in Nicaragua

Like many other Latin American countries, Nicaragua retains many of the customs of old Spain. In the weeks leading up to Christmas, people stroll the streets where there are many things to purchase: toys, foods, candles, and Nativity pictures. Children carry fragrant bouquets to the altar of the Virgin and sing carols. Church bells beckon the people to Midnight Mass on Christmas Eve. Oftentimes the holiday season concludes with a brilliant display of fireworks.

Christmas in Brazil

Christmas is celebrated in a deeply religious way throughout South America. The central focus of the season on the continent is the *presepio* — "the manger." Oftentimes an entire room is devoted to the manger display, complete with landscape and tiny figures to scale. Though the main focus is the manger at Bethlehem, the intricate scenes may include hills full of shepherds gazing upon the heavenly host, the Wise Men crossing the desert on their camels, water mills, small caves, electric trains, or even sailboats at sea.

The people of northern Brazil enjoy a version of the folk play *Los Pastores* — "The Shepherds." In the Brazilian version there are shepherdesses rather than shepherds. There is also a Gypsy who attempts to kidnap the Christ child.

Christmas in Chile

Christmas in Chile is celebrated in accordance with most of the region but features two unique events. In Andacollo there is a grand festival honoring the Virgin Mary. It is similar to a country fair, and features horse racing. The gift-giver in Chile is *Viejo Pascuero* — "Old Man Christmas" —who oddly enough is transported by reindeer.

Christmas in Colombia

Part of the Colombian Christmas tradition closely resembles American Halloween festivities. On Christmas Eve people dress up in costumes and roam the streets. Those who can guess the true identity behind a mask are given a gift. Colombia is also one of the few Latin countries in which children receive gifts brought by the Christ child on Christmas Eve instead of on Epiphany.

Christmas in Venezuela

Between December 16 and 24, Venezuelans attend a daily *Misa de Aguinaldo* or "early morning mass." In the capital city of

Caracas, it is customary to roller skate to this service. Thus many neighborhoods close the streets to cars until 8 a.m. At bedtime, children tie one end of a piece of string to their big toe and hang the other end out the window. The next morning, rollers skaters give a tug to any string they see hanging. After mass everyone looks forward to tostados and coffee.

Christmas in Bethlehem

Every year at Christmas, thousands of Christians make a pilgrimage to Bethlehem, the town where Jesus was born and the site of the Church of the Nativity. The festivities in the "little town" center on the Church which is always ablaze with flags and decorations, as well as the Shepherds' Fields, which represent the fields where the angels announced the arrival of Christ. The Church of the Nativity is believed to stand on the place where Christ was born.

On Christmas Eve, residents and visitors alike crowd the church's doorway and stand on the roof to watch the dramatic annual procession. Police mounted on Arabian horses lead the parade, followed by a solitary horseman carrying a cross and sitting astride a coal-black steed. Then come the government and church officials. The procession solemnly enters the doors and places an ancient effigy of the Christ child inside. Visitors can climb down a set of deep winding stairs that lead to a cavern, where a silver star can be found marking the place where Mary gave birth to Jesus.

Christian homes in Bethlehem are marked by a cross painted over the door. Each house displays a homemade manger scene and a star is set up on a pole in the village square. The Roman Catholics in Bethlehem celebrate Christmas on December 25, the Greek Orthodox on January 6, and the Armenian Christians on January 18. Representatives protecting the interests of these three groups sit on a board that "governs" the Church of the Nativity, so that no one group will be favored or slighted. There are no services held within the church itself; rather they are held in an adjoining building. Services on Christmas Eve are by invitation only but are televised to the crowds outside. After the service most people venture to the Shepherds' Fields, which also are divided into three sections.

Christmas in Iran

Formerly Persia, Iran is the land where the Wise Men are believed to have lived when Jesus was born. Today, Christians in Iran begin fasting from animal products on December 1. This is commonly called the "Little Fast," as compared to the "Big Fast" that occurs during Lent. After attending church on December 25, Iranians enjoy a special Christmas dinner that they call "Little Feast." A customary dish is a chicken stew called *harasa*. Gifts are not exchanged, but children usually get new clothes, which they proudly wear on Christmas Day.

Christmas in Iraq

On Christmas Eve, Christian families in Iraq gather together and one of the children reads aloud about the birth of Jesus while other family members hold lighted candles. After the reading is finished, a bonfire of thorn bushes is lit and everyone sings. If the thorns burn to ashes, good luck will be granted for the coming year. When the fire dies, each family member jumps over the ashes three times and makes a wish.

Another bonfire is lit on Christmas day in the church yard. Carrying a figure of the baby Jesus, the bishop leads the service. Afterwards he blesses one person with the "touch of peace." That person touches the person next to them and the "touch" is passed around until all who are present have felt the touch of peace.

Christmas in Your World

After learning about how people celebrate Christmas in their corner of the world, you might want to add some of their ideas to your family's observance of the holiday. But no matter what you do, always keep *Christ* as the main focus of your celebration. He is the One who started it all, and He can enable us to experience the joy of Christmas 365 days a year.

Part Two:

What Happened to the Innocence of Christmas?

4

The Christmas Rush

No sooner does Thanksgiving end than the shopping frenzy for Christmas begins. In fact the last few years, retailers have begun promoting Christmas sales right after Halloween. Almost hourly, it seems, reporters alert us to the dwindling number of shopping days before December 25. And like herds of animals we blindly head to the malls, grumbling all the way about the terrible traffic, sullen crowds, and corrosive commercialism. Once inside the glittering bazaars, we push our credit cards and our patience to the limits, revealing very little of the Christmas joy in the process. After hours of searching and buying, we return home battered, weary, and dazed, suffering from P.S.S. (post-timorous shopping syndrome).

Christmas is the number one retailing holiday in America— but it hasn't always been this way. According to Daniel Boorstin, in his book *The Americans,* Christmas was mainly a non-event in America until the 1860s. It was in 1867 that Macy's Department Store remained open until midnight on Christmas Eve. A few years later, in 1874, Macy's produced its first window displays with Christmas themes. And from there the day has grown into a major retail holiday.

Retail Madness

Retail madness dates back to the 1940s. During World War II, it became necessary for Americans to mail their Christmas gifts early for the troops overseas to receive them in time. Merchants readily joined in the effort to remind the public to shop early. Thus the prolonged shopping season was born. During the 1940s, Chicago's Marshall Field & Company began to turn its huge department store into a "glittering fairyland" at Christmastime. Each year the company came up with a secret new theme for its decorations. Ever since that time, retail merchants have been hard at work to intensify our retail rituals during the holiday season.

To expand their profits, many stores made Thanksgiving the official springboard for Christmas sales. Still others started as early as Halloween. Gimbels, in Philadelphia, organized the first Thanksgiving Day parade in 1920, and featured Santa Claus as the main attraction. In 1924, both Macy's Department Store in New York and Hudson's in Detroit followed suit.

Unfortunately, the Great Depression brought retail sales to a near standstill. In 1939, after several years of Depression-deflated sales, the head of Federated Department Stores in Ohio argued that by advancing the date of Thanksgiving one week, an additional six days of shopping could be added. Supposedly convinced by this man's rationale, President Franklin Roosevelt moved Thanksgiving that year from November 30 to November 23. In 1941, Congress set the annual date of Thanksgiving as the fourth Thursday in November, thus guaranteeing a four-week shopping season each year. America's recognition of Christmas as a powerful economic force had reached new levels.

Just the Facts

Consider some of the statistics about our Christmas celebration:

- Ninety-six percent of Americans say they celebrate Christmas in some form.

- Seventy percent of Americans—including 62 percent of those who attend church regularly—say they consider Christmas the most significant Christian holiday.

- Eighty percent of Americans decorate for Christmas.

- More than 36 million Americans have real Christmas trees.

- The weeks leading up to Christmas are the biggest shopping weeks of the year. Many retailers make up to 50 percent of their annual income in the month preceding Christmas.

- Americans spent more than $500 billion last year on gifts. This makes the American Christmas larger than the gross national product of Ireland.

Of course this spending figure could drastically change if more people followed the "Ultimate Gift Guide" produced by the Robb Report. When a bathrobe, sweater or coffee maker just won't do, Robb Report magazine has come up with dozens of Christmas gift ideas that offer elegance and exclusivity. Here are a few of their suggestions, featured in the fifteenth annual report, listed for those who are willing to pay the premium: a custom $319,000 Bentley; an $18 million corporate jet; a 69-carat yellow-diamond bracelet designed by Florida's Greenleaf and Crosby jewelers; a $135,000 Chevrolet suburban, complete with computer, home theatre system, and satellite navigation; and for $295,000, a 3-foot-long sterling silver replica of the *Titanic*. (This offer, exclusively to readers of the luxury lifestyle magazine, includes a two-night trip for two to London to pick up the ship at the Asprey & Garrard showroom.) The total value of the gift package was $110 million. The average income of a Robb Report reader is $750,000, with an average net worth of $3.7 million. So maybe it's time to return to simpler days of gift buying.

You had better think twice about buying your true love all the gifts listed in the popular Christmas carol "The Twelve Days of Christmas." Rebekah McCahan, an investment strategist for PNC Bank Corporation, has been tallying up the costs of the "Twelve

Days of Christmas" for the last dozen years. While the prices of many goods and services have been falling lately, the items in the song will cost 6.5 percent more than last year. It's not that the prices for the birds—partridges, swans, doves, and geese—have gone up all that much; but it now costs a lot more for dancers, pear trees, and musicians.

Here's the cost of those gifts today, as compiled by McCahan:

- Partridge — $15.00
- Pear tree — $89.99
- Two turtle doves — $50.00
- Three French hens — $15.00
- Four calling birds — $280.00
- Five gold rings — $250.00
- Six geese-a-laying — $150.00
- Seven swans-a-swimming — $3,500.00
- Eight maids-a-milking — $41.20 (per hour, minimum wage)
- Nine ladies dancing — $3,932.72 (per performance)
- Ten lords-a-leaping — $3,433.99 (per performance)
- Eleven pipers piping — $1,179.36 (per performance)
- Twelve drummers drumming — $1,277.64 (per performance)

The cost of all the gifts—if you purchase them repeatedly on each day as the song suggests—is a wallet-busting $58,405.09!

Cyber-shopping

Any discussion of the Christmas rush would be incomplete without a look at cyber-shopping. Forget about the crowds, traffic, and ugly battles for sold-out toys—now millions of shoppers have turned to cyberspace for holiday gift-giving. After many years of failing to live up to unrealistic promises, e-commerce—buying over the Internet—is finally beginning to take off. Across America, catalogs are being replaced by URLs, cash registers are being overtaken by secure transaction proprieties, and merry ho-ho-ho's give way to a variety of error messages as people "surf the

Net" to procure presents. It won't be long before having a "White Christmas" is replaced by having a "Web Christmas."

Last year Americans spent an estimated $2.3 billion on Web gifts, which is only a fraction of the total holiday dollar drop. However, this is well over double the previous year's total. Some people are predicting a threefold increase in Christmas e-sales in the future. According to Jupiter Communications, almost 17 million people bought something from a Website in 1998, up from 10 million in 1997 and 5 million in 1996. Within a decade, the Jupiter people believe, mouse-clickers will eclipse catalog buyers.[3] Even "America's Homemaker" Martha Stewart believes that the future for her company lies in online shopping.

The most successful Websites offer you a quick means to get to the merchandise and easy personalization. Savings are also important, especially since the Web encourages swift comparisons. For some small retail merchants, this just adds to the pressure they are already under in competing for customers, though other small businesses have found success in partnering with shopping super-sites like Microsoft, Yahoo, and AOL. However, cyber-merchants do have advantages small businesses do not have, like low overhead and unlimited shelf space.

While shopping online offers savings, convenience, and a fool-proof way to avoid crowds and elevator music, it does have annoying drawbacks as well. Despite its rapid development, e-shopping is definitely a work in progress. Even its most enthusiastic supporters have to endure some unpleasant pitfalls. There can be frustrating long waits, especially if you don't know what you want and have to browse, searching for just the right gift. Then there are the limited payment options. If a site doesn't take credit cards, then it's back to the land of "snail mail." Getting a question answered online is often a hit-and-miss proposition, creating customer service gaps. There also are concerns regarding fraud and privacy that are still being resolved with e-shopping.

Avoiding the Christmas Rush

Despite the fact that many people are caught in the Christmas rush trap, there are growing numbers of people who are re-thinking how to participate in this holiday. Consider the results of a poll taken of Americans regarding the commercial and spiritual aspects of Christmas.[4]

- Many Americans think Christmas is too commercial, and 48 percent say the Santa Claus tradition and gift-giving detract from the religious celebration.

- 44 percent of Americans think they spend too much money on gifts at Christmas while 48 percent say they spend just the right amount.

- The spiritual aspect of the holiday is important to many Americans since 82 percent agree that "Christmas is a time of reflection for me."

If we are going to survive the confusion, frustration, and uncertainty that occur at Christmastime, we need to be willing to make some changes. A few simple guidelines can make the holiday gift-giving process a lot easier.

First, *help your family develop a gift-giving plan in advance for the year.* Make sure that everyone has a calendar listing all the events during the year that require gifts. The calendar is not only a good reminder for birthdays and other occasions, but it becomes a great tool to help save for presents as well. Make sure that each member of the family understands the importance of appropriate gift-giving.

A family meeting can be a good place to start. Guidelines can be set for gift-giving spending limits. Older children could be allowed to spend more, and younger ones could receive a "matching amount" from parents for their purchases. Pooling money for a larger gift can also work well. A good way to help children understand the value of money is to have them calculate the cost of their Christmas "wish list." They could be easily surprised at the steep cost of their own list!

Second, *encourage family members to be creative in their gift-giving.* Do some detective work when visiting relatives. Try and find out favorite colors or collections that have been started, or even gain a sense for items that would make practical gifts. Better yet, create homemade gifts. Personal creations become special one-of-a-kind gifts that are enjoyed by everyone. Family members could also give "personal service" gifts. These can be as simple as colored strips of paper with a message written on them, placed in a decorative jar. The messages could be things like "good for one day of weeding" or "good for one car wash." You are only limited by your imagination!

Third, *remember that knowing how to receive can be as important as knowing how to give a gift.* Children should learn it is the thought that counts when he or she gets gifts as well as gives them. Even if the gift doesn't appeal to the child—a toy that is too juvenile or clothes they consider "uncool"—he or she can still respond in a positive way. "This is great, thanks for thinking of me," expresses appreciation to the giver. We also have made it a practice with our children to have them send notes or handmade thank you cards in appreciation for gifts received.

Fourth, *take some time individually and as a family to decide what you are going to give Jesus for His birthday.* Discuss how you can use gifts, talents, and abilities to offer a special present to the Lord, not just at Christmas but throughout the year. Look for ways your family can reach out to others in your neighborhood or to your extended family with the true message of Christmas.

5

Whatever Happened to Christmas Vacation?

A few years ago the Lutheran Hour ministries commissioned Emmy winner Wang Films Ltd. to produce a show called "Red Boots for Christmas," a half-hour cartoon based on a German folk tale with a Christmas message. Their objective was to educate and remind children and parents about the genuine story of Christmas.

The cartoon does precisely that. It tells of a gruff, friendless cobbler named Hans who lives in a tiny German village. Just before Christmas, an angel appears to him and tells him to make a gift for God. The angel promises that God will in turn give him an even more valuable gift. Hans uses his finest red leather to make a pair of boots, and in the process he becomes a more loving and kinder human being. However, on Christmas Eve, he is sad and disillusioned because God has not arrived with His gift.

As he waits, Hans sees a poor girl walking barefoot across the snow. Suddenly he realizes that God means for him to give the red boots to the girl, which he promptly does. Then he wonders where he'll find God's return gift. As the *burgermeister* in the story explains, "We give to each other because God has given us the greatest gift of all." At that point, Hans understands the gift the angel promised is the Christ child.

In this half-hour cartoon, the Lutheran Church makes a point important to a full understanding of Christmas: *Christians give presents to one another because God gave His Son to the world.* Unfortunately, such a reminder of the meaning and origin of Christmas gift-giving was disturbing to the major television networks. All of them rejected the show, even when the Lutherans offered to buy advertising time to finance the entire half-hour.

Who was ultimately responsible for this decision? Maybe we should blame the network executives, or possibly corporate America, which buys advertising from the networks. But the reality is the answer lies much deeper than this. Western culture is simply no longer interested in the truth about Christmas. We are living in a society that has been gradually moving away from Judeo-Christian values and becoming pluralistic. We seem to be on a course to remove God from every dimension of societal life, from commerce to education.

No More Merry Christmas

Take for example, shopping at a mall or department store at Christmastime. The stores are jammed with shoppers buying presents. Cash registers are ringing and merchants are wrapping presents. Customers are streaming through the doors loaded down with packages. It's all standard behavior for this time of year. But in most malls and stores you can search in vain for an important word—Christmas. It is basically nowhere to be found, yet a few years ago it would have been everywhere.

There are no banners with "Peace on Earth, Good Will to Men." Few manger scenes. Wise men are absent, and there's hardly a star to be found. Few stores wish their customers "Merry Christmas" with a banner. Christmas trees are plentiful, but somehow most department store and mall decorators omit any explicitly Christian allusions. Many of the stores use holly wreaths and swags of fir and spruce branches, hung with brightly colored ornaments, but allow no reference to the birth of the Savior.

Big department stores seem to be carefully avoiding Christmas rhetoric in producing their "holiday slogans." In a way they are helping the world to forget that December is the month in which the birth of Jesus Christ is celebrated. Nieman-Marcus, filled with beautiful decorations minus any Christian references, coined the phrase "Nieman-Marcus Unwrapped." Montgomery Ward, much less elaborately decorated, chose the new cry of the season— "Happy Holidays."

This is all quite deliberate. It is an attempt by commercial America to obliterate the memory of Christmas—custom by custom, image by image, word by word. Why? The biggest reason has to do with the age of tolerance in which we are living. No one wants to offend anybody, so they cut out references to Christ. More and more it appears that the very existence of Christianity seems to pose increasing problems for those making an attempt to manage our society. One place this is becoming apparent is in our educational system.

No More "Christmas" Vacation

In the last few years there has been a conscious effort to remove God from our public schools, even when it comes to Christmas. One example of this is changing "Christmas vacation" to "Winter break." Traditional carols mentioning Christ are said to violate students' rights and are no longer permitted to be sung by student choral groups.

New Age philosophies and eastern Mysticism are being brought into our classrooms, while God is being shown the exit door. Even Halloween is celebrated in some form on most school campuses, but Christmas is being rejected as "too Christian" for our public schools. Education has become a battlefield for a wide array of causes and issues, including school-based clinics, values clarification, evolution, self-esteem, and gay awareness. Meanwhile the dropout rate continues to increase, and we are just beginning to wake up to the literacy problem.

During hearings held by the U.S. Department of Education on proposed regulations for the Protection of Pupil Rights Amendment, more than 1300 pages of testimony were recorded by court reporters as public school teachers, parents, and concerned adults recounted the psychological abuse of children in the public school system. Accounts were given of how classroom instruction had confused kids about life, standards of behavior, moral choices, religious beliefs, and relationships with peers and parents.[5] Kids are being alienated from their parents and traditional morality, while being taught to rationalize rather than discern. Without question, we've come a long way since the days of the "little red schoolhouse."

Abraham Lincoln said, "The philosophy of education in one generation will be the philosophy of government in the next." Public education influences the greatest number of people, in the most thorough way, at the most impressionable age. Just what philosophy are our children being taught in the classroom today? What values are they assimilating to help them deal with the trials of life? Instead of talking about God, children are introduced to "spirits." Instead of celebrating Christmas, children are being indoctrinated into the celebration of occultism.

Concerned parents across America are rising up to take action against the significant inroads into the educational system that the occult and the New Age movement have made. One cannot completely comprehend the impact this movement is having on the educational process until one understands the many faces the New Age is wearing in schools today. The real purpose behind exposing school children to the occult was summed up by a teacher attending a New Age seminar: "To help the children get in touch with their divinity. These things are crucial to our own evolution."[6]

A New Age in the Classroom

The U.S. Army Research Institute asked the National Research Council to form a committee to assess the field of techniques that purport to enhance human performance. The committee's members were drawn from The National Academy of Sciences & Engineering and the Institute of Medicine.

Many of the techniques under consideration grew out of the human potential movement of the 1960s, including guided imagery, meditation, biofeedback, neurolinguistic programming, and various other techniques to reduce stress and increase concentration.[7] The Army, like many other institutions, is attracted to the prospect of cost-effective procedures that can improve performance. Educators are looking for the very same thing to enhance classroom performance, and New Age researchers are all too anxious to install their methodology in the classroom. Let's take a brief look at some of the things that are transpiring in classrooms today.

Schools are gradually replacing education that addresses a child's intellect by teaching knowledge and skills (cognitive) with education that targets the child's feelings and attitudes, spending classroom time on psychological games (affective). This new direction has been dubbed "therapy" education by some. A new jargon was even designed by those who promote therapy education. This educational language includes phrases like "values clarification," "behavior modification," "moral reasoning," "higher critical thinking skills," and "holistic education." Techniques associated with these phrases are being carefully integrated into school curriculum. New Age methodology like yoga, meditation, and globalism is being masked by terminology that doesn't sound quite so strange or threatening, so as to not alarm parents and to hide the truth of what is being taught.

This seeming "innocence" of New Age terminology helps to make the basic ideas much more readily acceptable. New Age activist Dick Stuphen states: "One of the biggest advantages we have as New Agers is once the occult, metaphysical, and New Age terminology is removed, we have concepts and techniques that are very acceptable to the general public. So we can change the names to demonstrate the power. In doing so, we open the door to millions who normally would not be receptive."[8]

According to Professor Allan Bloom, "courses in value-clarification teach kids to discover and clarify their own values rather than having them imposed by outside authority. Those that are springing up in schools are supposed to provide models for parents and encourage kids to talk about things like abortion or sexism—issues the significance of which they can not possibly understand. Such education is little more than propaganda. Propaganda that does not work, because the opinions or values arrived at are will-o'-the wisps, insubstantial, without ground in experience or passion, which are the basis for moral reasoning. Such values inevitably change as public opinion changes."[9] Values clarification is compatible with New Age thinking on "confluent education." This New Age theory posits the equality of individual values because everyone has the wisdom of the universe within. New Age proponent and actress Shirley MacLaine puts it this way: "We already know everything. The knowingness of our divinity is the highest intelligence."[10]

In many cases, teachers are being encouraged to transform their classrooms into laboratories to "experiment" on children rather than to emphasize basic life skills. Kids are at a crucial stage of life where values, perspectives, and morals are under attack from TV, the print media, the Internet, and in their own classroom. What was once supposed to be a "safe haven of learning" has turned into an "occultic minefield of indoctrination and conversion." Transcendental meditation practices are now being used under the guise of increasing self-esteem. Astrologers, palm readers, channelers, and even Tibetan monks are being invited to come into classrooms to "challenge students"—all in the name of critical thinking and understanding a different world view. Yet because of the mandate to keep church and state separate, Christians are not allowed to present their views on campus. I spend considerable time each year on public campuses in North America doing assemblies, and I am continually reminded not to mention God, Jesus, or the Bible in my presentation. Sometimes I wonder what people are afraid of when it comes to the Christ of Christmas.

Teachers are being shown how they can make use of fantasy role-playing games like "Magic: The Gathering" to enhance performance. One similar game, "The Wizard," is being played in some classrooms as part of the actual curriculum. In the game, kids are taught to cast spells on each other. The described purpose of "The Wizard" is to progress from one "spelling power" level to the next. Humans are at the lowest end of the spectrum, having very limited powers, and are at the mercy of monsters. Higher levels include enchanters, sorcerers, magicians, and of course the Wizard.

In some schools kids are routinely sent to the school counselor's office to lie on the floor and breathe deeply. Then they meditate as they listen to a series of guided fantasy tapes, while they empty their minds and at times are even led to participate in astral projection.[11]

Textbooks and Curriculum

Long gone are the days of "Dick and Jane." No longer are primary school children being taught to read from innocent materials. They have been replaced with books containing stories that promote fear, violence, and occultic themes. This becomes even more horrifying when you realize the power these textbooks have to influence the vulnerable minds of our children. Seventy-five percent of students' classroom time and 90 percent of homework time is spent with textbook materials.[12]

The National Institute of Education commissioned a systematic study of the content of public school textbooks. The conclusion was quite alarming: "Religion, traditional family values, and conservative political and economic positions have been reliably excluded from the children's textbooks."[13] Any educator can tell you that omitting these values from textbooks sends a very definite message to children: "These values must be unimportant because they were omitted. They are of lesser value than those which were included."

New Age educators are developing and testing curriculum at a feverish pace in hopes of gaining broader acceptance in school districts across the country. In order to be approved, the curriculum is being cleverly disguised and packaged as brain research and "scientific" techniques to help develop creativity, enhance learning capacity, enable children to manage stress, solve problems, and improve their self-esteem. But the curriculum is sometimes nothing more than an advertisement for New Age thinking. For example, in the "Impressions" series, published by Holt Rinehart and Winston, the teacher's manual instructs the educator to assign children the task of composing a spell. They are to write and chant a spell to make things in the room float and then subsequently do the same thing to return the room to normal.[14]

Mission S.O.A.R. (Set Objectives, Achieve Results) was piloted in Los Angeles schools to help reduce gang violence and build self-esteem in kids. In the program, children are taught to "communicate with the dead" and receive "guidance" from their "spiritual guides" on how to plan their future lives.[15]

Children who are talented and gifted are a prime target for "conversion" to New Age philosophy. Because these programs are generally very open for experimentation, they become prime avenues for occult-oriented "transpersonal education."[16] "Flights of Fantasy" is a program used with gifted children. It is a form of guided imagery that trains children to imagine meeting strange creatures in space, then encourages the children to join or merge with them before returning to Earth.

There is no doubt that this material is damaging to young minds subjected to it under the guise of public education. As you closely examine some of these examples, you begin to realize that most of the content is too much for a young child's psyche to process. The frightening imagery overwhelms them, and they are being asked to deal with issues that they are ill equipped to handle. In the process of this kind of study, they are being desensitized to the things of the occult. It's this subtle desensitization that we must protect our kids against.

Dangers of New Age Philosophies in Education

Confluent education leads kids to believe that they are divine and perfect. Since the sin problem is nonexistent, there is no need for Jesus Christ and what He accomplished on the cross. Because they are taught they are "godlike," children can develop a false sense of confidence.

The utilization of guided imagery in the classroom teaches children a way of dealing with problems that leaves God out of the picture. It can also open us up to "angels of light," the false messengers mentioned in 2 Corinthians 11:14. New Age visualization is also dangerous because it denies the "lostness of man" and the problem of sin. Remember that our imaginations were also affected by the Fall (Genesis 6:5), so a mind allowed to run completely free will undoubtedly head toward sin and debasement, not righteousness and goodness.

Values clarification in the classroom denies the existence of moral absolutes, absolute truth, and the notion of right and wrong. Instead, each student is encouraged to come up with his or her own moral value system or "Ten Commandments." In essence, each child is instructed to become his or her own God.

Eastern meditation teaches one to empty the mind with the goal of attaining oneness with all things—a "cosmic consciousness." Biblical meditation is much different because it always has an objective focus: filling the mind with the Word of God.

With confluent education, guided imagery visualization, values clarification, Eastern meditation, and a variety of mystical and occultic curricula making their way into schools, it becomes clear that the New Age movement has made significant inroads into the educational system. Thus there are profound implications for Christian parents who have children in public schools, which often don't want to celebrate the birth of Jesus Christ, nor even allow it to be mentioned, but allow any other sort of religious expression.

Safeguarding Your Children

The apostle Paul encourages believers in 1 Corinthians 16:13-14 to "be on guard and stand firm in the faith" and to "do everything in love." It is important to keep these principles in mind as you develop a plan for safeguarding your child's public education experience. Here are some basic things to consider in the process.

First, *become informed.* It's been said the best defense is a good offense. The problem is that most parents don't have a clue as to what is going on in their children's schools. Start making a more conscious effort to find out what your child is being taught in the classroom. Contact your local school district office and ask what curriculum is being used. Ask permission to review the material for yourself. If your request is denied, file a complaint with the district office. And remember: always do your homework. Know what you are talking about—don't go to the school without a factual, well-thought-out defense. Make sure you earn the right to be heard by carefully relating your concerns based on the facts.

Second, *remain involved.* It's no longer enough to be involved in bake sales and open houses. Parents need to go beyond "meeting their obligations" by occasionally helping out at school or even going on field trips. I went on a field trip with Tony and Kati's seventh-grade class to Chinatown in Los Angeles. It was a very positive experience not only because I saw a whole different side of the students and teachers but because I got to spend some special time with my kids. Get into the classroom. Observe what is taking place. Inform the teacher and administration if you notice any questionable practices going on. Again, remember to "stand firm" but "do everything in love." It does take time, valuable time, but it's more than worth the investment.

Third, *secure help.* Seek out curriculum experts, child psychologists, teachers, other parents, pastors, and other leaders who share your views. Develop a united group of concerned adults and request a meeting with the district superintendent to discuss the curriculum and questionable activities you may be concerned about in the classroom. Be persistent. However, make every effort not to turn this into an "us against them" battle. Let educators know that you want the best for each child and support their position as teachers. Establish some common ground with them wherever possible. Remember these are very dedicated men and women teaching in schools today, and they need our encouragement and support. Most important, pray for your child, the teacher, and the situation that may need to be resolved. James 5:16 reminds us that the prayer of a righteous person is powerful and effective.

Fourth, *respond when necessary.* If the teacher, administration, or superintendent rejects or ignores your request, or if you have a one-sided, unproductive meeting, consider going to the school board. Prepare well and document everything in writing, with actual copies where possible. If it appears that harmful curriculum or practices will remain, request that alternative classes be established for children whose parents are opposed to the current course work. Ask that a parental review panel be established to monitor quality control in these alternative classes.

Let's do something before we lose another generation. Let's not allow the complacency of our society to subtly restrain us from protecting the most precious natural resource in our nation: our children. There is too much at stake, and we can ill afford to allow themes of despair, occultism, and witchcraft to deeply entrench themselves in the vulnerable minds of our kids. By all means, let's do everything we can to tell this generation the real reason for our holiday celebrations in December.

6

Touched by an Angel

There was a time when you encountered angels mainly in manger scenes and as Christmas ornaments. Maybe you grew up making "snow angels" by falling on your back in the snow and moving your arms up and down. And don't forget the parade of Top Ten musical hits over the years that have relied on angels—songs like "Earth Angel," "You Are My Special Angel," and the more contemporary hit by The Newsboys entitled "Entertaining Angels."

More recently, "angelmania" has infiltrated popular culture in a huge way. According to the Barna Research Group, three-quarters of all adults believe there are spiritual forces that we cannot see but that affect the material world in which we live. Baby boomers are the group most accepting of the unseen world.[17]

Angels are everywhere in mainstream culture, from ceramic figurines to the megahit on prime-time television, "Touched by an Angel." *Time* magazine put it this way:

> In the past few years angels have lodged in the popular imagination, celestial celebrities trailing clouds of glory as they come. There are angels-only boutiques, angel newsletters, angel seminars, angels on *Sonya Live*. A TIME poll indicates that most Americans believe in angels. Harvard Divinity School has a course on angels; Boston College has two. Bookstores had to establish angel sections. In the most celebrated

play on Broadway, Tony Kushner's Pulitzer-prize winning *Angels in America*, a divine messenger ministers to a man with AIDS. In *Publisher's Weekly's* religious bestseller list, five of ten books are about angels.[18]

In a similar way, *Newsweek* magazine declared, "angels are everywhere in America."[19] The article goes on to introduce those who claim to have talked to angels, tells of workshops that assist you in unleashing "your inner angel," and even describes angel focus groups! Angels are selling big time. There are angel calendars, figurines, T-shirts, postcards, jewelry, and sunglasses and a plethora of angel books. Sales are so hot that there are collectors clubs, catalog houses, and stores that sell nothing but angel merchandise.

What has given rise to the current angelmania that is sweeping our country? Ron Rhodes, in his book *Angels Among Us*, touches on some of the various reasons today's "angel experts" suggest for the rise in angel popularity:

- Angels ostensibly offer humankind a form of spirituality that does not involve commitment to God or the laws of God.

- Angels are supposedly a means of attaining God's help without having to deal directly with God.

- Angels have allegedly stepped up their activity among human beings in recent years in order to help them.

- Guardian angels are popular today because of people's perceived need for protection in an often threatening world.

- Angel worship is a reaction against the materialism and secularism of Western society.

- Angels are believed to bring meaning and purpose into our lives.

- Angels allegedly give assurance to all people regarding life after death.[20]

As you can see, most of the excitement people have today about angels is rooted in recklessly unbiblical ideas. In fact, much of what is being taught today about angels has more to do with fallen angels (demons) than God's holy angels.

The Bible is the only authoritative source from which we can acquire knowledge about angels and other spiritual matters. God is the creator of angels (Colossians 1:16), and He is the One who can tell us the real facts we need to know about them.

Are Angels for Real?

Dr. S.W. Mitchell, a celebrated Philadelphia neurologist, had gone to bed after an exceptionally tiring day. Suddenly he was awakened by someone knocking on his door. Opening it, he found a little girl, poorly dressed and deeply upset. She told him her mother was very sick and asked if he would please come with her. It was a bitterly cold, snowy night, but though he was bone tired, Dr. Mitchell dressed and followed the girl.

He found the mother desperately ill with pneumonia. After arranging for medical care, he complimented the sick woman on the intelligence and persistence of her little daughter. The woman looked at him strangely and said, "My daughter died a month ago." She added, "Her shoes and coat are in the clothes closet there." Mitchell, amazed and perplexed, went to the closet and opened the door. There hung the very coat worn by the little girl who had brought him to tend to her mother. It was warm and dry and could not possibly have been worn in the wintry night.[21]

Could the doctor have been called in the hour of desperate need by an angel who appeared as this woman's daughter? Was this the work of God's angels on behalf of the sick woman?

Reverend John G. Paton was a missionary in the New Hebrides Islands. Hostile natives surrounded his mission headquarters one night, intent on burning the Patons out and killing them. John Paton and his wife prayed all during that terror-filled night that God would deliver them. When daylight came they were amazed to see the attackers unaccountably leave. They thanked God for delivering them.

A year later, the chief of the tribe was converted to Jesus Christ, and Mr. Paton, remembering what had happened, asked the chief what had kept him and his men from burning down the house and killing them. The chief replied in surprise, "Who were all those men you had with you there?" The missionary told him there had been no men there, only himself and his wife. The chief argued that they had seen many men standing guard—hundreds of big men in shining garments with drawn swords in their hands. They seemed to circle the mission station so that the natives were afraid to attack. Only then did Mr. Paton realize that God had sent His angels to protect them. The chief agreed that there was no other explanation. Could it be that God had sent a legion of angels to protect His servants, whose lives were being endangered?[22]

God in the Bible clearly reveals there can be no question about the existence of angels. There are more than 100 references to angels in the Old Testament, while the New Testament mentions them about 165 times. Their existence is mentioned in thirty-four books of the Bible (seventeen in the Old Testament and seventeen in the New Testament) from the earliest (Job) to the last (Revelation). The teaching of Jesus includes a number of references to angels as real beings, so to deny their existence is to cast doubt on His truthfulness.

The fact is, angels are ambassadors of God. They belong to His heavenly court and service. Angels are created beings according to Psalm 148:5. They did not evolve from some lower or less complicated form of life. They cannot procreate for Matthew 22:30 tells us that at the resurrection, people will be like angels, neither marrying nor being given in marriage. The Bible does not specifically state the time of their creation, but since they were present when the earth was created (Job 38:7) their creation had to be before the creation of the earth.

Originally all angelic creatures were created holy, but Revelation 12:4 reveals that when sin entered the world, one-third of all the angels joined Satan, rebelled against God, and became demons. God's good angels—the ones who did not rebel against Him—are called holy in Mark 8:38.

Angels are distinct from human beings. As creatures they are limited in knowledge, power, and activity (1 Peter 1:11-12; Revelation 7:1), and like all responsible creatures, will be subject to judgment (see Matthew 25:41; 1 Corinthians 6:3; 1 Peter 1:11-12; and Revelation 7:1).

What Are Angels Like?

In Hebrews 1:14 angels are called "spirit beings," suggesting that they do not have tangible bodies. Consequently they do not function as human beings nor are they subject to death like we are. They do not have the same limitations people do. Angels have greater power and wisdom than we do, although these still are limited by God.

However, angels are limited, compared to man, in other ways. Since they are not created in the image of God, they cannot share in our magnificent destiny of salvation in Christ. At the end of the age, believers in Christ will be exalted above angels, according to 1 Corinthians 6:3.

Usually angels appear as men and have appeared in dreams and visions (Matthew 1:20; Isaiah 6:1-8), in special manifestations of their presence (2 Kings 6:17), and to people in a normal, conscious, waking state (Genesis 19:1-8; Mark 16:5). Some angels do have wings (Isaiah 6:2,6) and in some heavenly visions they possess superhuman characteristics.

Angels constitute a huge number which cannot be counted, according to Revelation 5:11, and there is a vast organization and ranking of angels. The Bible speaks of the "council" and the "assembly" of angels (Psalm 89:5,7), of their organization for battle (Revelation 12:7) and even of various ranks of angels—archangels, chief princes, governmental rulers, cherubim, and seraphim. Without a doubt, God has organized the good angels and Satan has organized the evil ones. Only Michael is designated as the archangel, or high-ranking angel (Jude 9:1; 1 Thessalonians 4:16). He leads the angelic armies of heaven against Satan and forces of evil, and in the book of Daniel he appears as the guardian angel of Israel who will be of special help during her time of trouble.

Other prominent individual angels are mentioned in the Bible, one of which is Gabriel. Gabriel's name means "hero of God," and he appears to be a high-ranking angel. His function has been to bring important messages from God to several individuals. Gabriel is important to the Christmas story because he is the one who told Mary that the One born to her would be great and would rule on the throne of David (Luke 1:26-27). Lucifer (Satan) was an anointed cherub. He fell from his original exalted position and led a host of angels, one-third of all angels, from heaven in his rebellion against God (Ezekiel 28:16-17; Revelation 12:4).

The Ministry of Angels

Good angels are essentially servants. Hebrews 1:14 says, "Are not all angels ministering spirits sent to serve those who will inherit salvation?" Besides their ministry to believers, angels also have a ministry to God, and they even have a relationship to unbelievers.

Their primary ministry to God is to worship and praise Him. The cherubim defend His holiness, while the seraphim surround His throne and attend to His holiness. The Bible also tells us angels praise Him (Isaiah 6:3), worship Him (Revelation 5:8-13), rejoice in what He does (Job 38:6-7), serve Him (Psalm 103:20), and act as instruments of His judgment (Revelation 7:1; 8:2). Angels also seem to be very active when God institutes a new era in history. For example, angels joined in praise when the earth was created (Job 38:6-7), they were involved in the giving of the Mosaic Law (Galatians 3:19; Hebrews 2:2), and they were active during the early years of the Church (Acts 8:26; 10:3,7; 12:11).

In addition, angels have a significant ministry to Christ, from before His birth until His second coming. Just as angelic beings surround the throne of the Father, so the angels also attend to God the Son. Gabriel informed Mary of the birth of Christ (Luke 1:26-28), an angel announced the birth of Christ to the shepherds and was then accompanied in praise by a multitude of other angels (Luke 2:8-15), and angels protected Jesus in infancy. It was an angel that warned Joseph and Mary to flee Egypt to escape Herod's wrath (Matthew 2:13-15), and an angel that instructed the couple when it was safe to return to the land of Israel (Matthew 2:20).

Angels encouraged Jesus after the forty days of temptation (Matthew 4:11), and strengthened Him in His stress at Gethsemane (Luke 22:43). The Lord Himself declared that a legion of angels stood ready to come to His defense if called on (Matthew 26:53).

It was an angel that rolled away the stone from Christ's tomb (Matthew 28:1-2), announced His resurrection to the women on that first Easter morning (Luke 24:5-7), and reminded the women of Jesus' earlier promise to rise on the third day. Angels also were present at Jesus' ascension (Acts 1:10-11), and will prepare the world for and participate in the second coming of Jesus Christ.

Angels have a unique relationship to unbelievers, for they will be involved in carrying out judgment. They announce impending judgments to unbelievers (Genesis 19:13; Revelation 14:6-7), inflict those judgments on the unrighteous (Acts 12:23), and will separate the righteous from the unrighteous (Matthew 13:39-40).

God's angels have also been commissioned and sent out with the responsibility of aiding believers. They minister to us personally, offering encouragement, protection, and provision at the Lord's behest. When Paul was caught in a storm at sea, an angel encouraged him, reminding Paul that he would arrive safely in Rome to be a witness for Christ (Acts 27:23-25). It was an angel that protected David when he was forced to flee the Philistines

(Psalm 34:7), and an angel offered Elijah nourishment when he was weak in the midst of a lengthy journey (1 Kings 19:5-7).

Philip received direction from an angel to witness to the Ethiopian official (Acts 8:26), and an angel arranged the meeting of Cornelius and Peter that resulted in many coming to Christ (Acts 10:3,22). There appears to be a connection between the prayer for Peter's release from prison and the angel's releasing him (Acts 12:1-11), and in a similar way, Daniel's prayer was explained by an angel (Daniel. 9: 20-27).

Angels aid in winning people to Christ (Acts 8:26; 10:3), and care for the righteous at the time of death. Luke 16:22 describes the death of Lazarus and the angels carrying him to Abraham's side.

Without question the most popular and controversial aspect of angels has to do with their role as the guardians of God's people. The idea of individual guardian angels is popular today among New Age angel enthusiasts, and there are some Bible scholars who say that every single believer has a personal guardian angel who stays with them throughout their life.

There are two main passages in the Bible that relate to the idea of guardian angels. Matthew 18:10 reads, "See that you do not look down on one of these little ones. For I tell you that their angels in heaven always see the face of my Father in heaven." The second passage is found in Acts 12:15. In this incident we find a servant girl named Rhoda recognizing Peter's voice outside the door of the house, and people inside—thinking Peter was still in jail—saying, "You're out of your mind." When she kept insisting it was so, they said, "It must be his angel." Quite a few Bible scholars have made the conclusion from these two verses that every believer must have a guardian angel. Whether each of us has just one angel watching over us or many we cannot know for sure, yet one thing is certain: We as Christians need to become more aware of God's provision of angelic protection. Regardless of how many angels are involved, we should become less fearful of our circumstances and our enemies. Imagine how different our lives would be if we could recognize God's constant provision of angelic protection.

As believers, let's be encouraged. Angels are closer than we think. There are millions of angels who are at God's command to help you with the issues of life in the twenty-first century. Take heart that God has "commanded his angels concerning you to guard you in all your ways; they will lift you up in their hands so that you will not strike your foot against a stone" (Psalm 91:11-12).

Part Three:

What's
a Christian
to Do?

7

A Look at the Book

The true meaning of Christmas concerns the most amazing event in human history, yet somehow this message is easily lost in the gift-buying frenzy and the storefront Santa Claus. Add to this the endless advice on how to make this "the best Christmas ever" and you've got major confusion. This ignorance about the meaning of Christmas is rampant, even among Christians. Some say "Bah! Humbug!" to Santa, while others sound like the Grinch who stole Christmas when it comes to decorating evergreen trees. Whom should you listen to?

Knowing how to respond to contemporary culture issues can be perplexing and frustrating at times. Everyone has an opinion as to what is the best thing for Christians to do. After being interviewed hundreds of times in the last couple of years on various radio and television programs, I am convinced that I have heard the best and worst advice people have to offer on a variety of subjects. The bottom line in responding to any issue is not what other people think, no matter how dogmatic they may be. What matters is what God thinks; and what He says in His Word.

The Bible is God's handbook for living, and as such contains truth by which we are able to examine issues in contemporary culture...like the right way to celebrate Christmas. That's why it is important to take a "look at the book." There are no chapters and verses you can turn to that specifically mention Santa Claus, reindeer, Christmas trees, or candy canes. Yet there are solid principles that, if applied properly, can enable us to respond to the issue of keeping Christ in Christmas in a way that pleases God and is still fun for the members of our family.

Principles for Keeping the Right Focus at Christmas

If we were living back in the 1940s or '50s, we would experience vastly different Christmas celebrations than we do today. Without a doubt, times have changed. Today it's hard to weed through the heavy commercialization and keep the focus on what should be a very special time of year. Should Santa Claus be part of your family's holiday celebration? Is it okay for Christians to have Christmas trees in their homes? What about exchanging gifts? These and other Christmastime issues need thoughtful attention. Rather than attempt to speculate about the "right way" to celebrate Christmas, let's take a look at some timeless guiding principles from God's Word.

First, remember that *not everything is constructive*. God has given each one of us a free will—essentially the freedom to choose. Knowing how far to exercise this liberty can sometimes be difficult to determine, especially on things about which the Bible is silent in terms of right and wrong. The apostle Paul addresses this issue with the Corinthian church in the New Testament: "Some of you say, 'We can do whatever we want to!' But I tell you that not everything we do is good or helpful" (1 Corinthians 10:23 CEV).

As Christians we have freedom in all things, including those things not specifically mentioned in the Bible as being sinful. However, this freedom must be exercised in such a way as to build up our spiritual life and encourage others. Whatever contributes to spiritual growth is good and helpful. We must be careful when it comes to questionable things, the gray areas of Christian living that are not specifically forbidden in the Bible. Sometimes these gray areas have to do with contemporary culture issues like traditions in celebrating Christmas.

It's easy to claim that believers should not get caught up in the commercial machine of Christmas, but with all the commercialization that takes place, we are provided with a good opportunity to "turn on the light" of God's Word and reveal the true meaning of Christmas to those around us. I believe Christians can participate in traditions like Santa Claus and Christmas trees, so long as we keep the focus on Christ. Of course, for some traditions, your decision will be based on what you as a family are comfortable with. But in Christ we have the freedom to participate or *not* participate in things like trees and Santa. We should also have the grace to allow other families to make their own decisions on what they'll do.

Second, *we should not conform to the world's behavior and customs.* Advertisers and retailers pull out all the stops at Christmastime. Consumerism reaches an annual high, and holiday decorations abound for all to see and enjoy, yet Jesus is almost nowhere to be found. How easy it has become to leave out the guest of honor at His own birthday. It is critical for followers of Christ to be wise in what customs of the world we adopt at Christmastime. In Romans 12:2, we are encouraged to not conform to the patterns of this world but instead be transformed by the renewing of our minds.

The patterns of this world are usually selfish and at times corrupting, even at Christmas. Our refusal to conform to the world, however, must go even deeper than rejecting Santa or refusing to put up a tree. Our commitment to Christ and our love for Him must be evident in all we do. Only when our minds are renewed by the new attitude the Lord gives us are we truly transformed. If our character is like Christ's, we can be sure our behavior will honor God. Once we have this new attitude, our approach to observing Christmas will change. That doesn't mean we will reject the traditional Christmas customs but that we will find ourselves incorporating them in new and different ways.

We must make it a priority to read God's Word, pray for direction, and apply its truth to our lives. Ask the Lord to help you escape the patterns of our society at Christmas. It takes practice, but it can be done. Work at keeping your family's attention and attitudes focused on the goodness of God's indescribable gift to us that very first Christmas. Your celebration of Christ's birth can still be fun, but you'll find it much more rewarding when Jesus is your motivation.

Third, *learn the benefits of giving*. So much of the focus of our society at Christmastime is on getting rather than on giving. Commercials endlessly bombard us with the "must-have items" for our Christmas wish lists as well as hints of what to give to that special someone. But how often do you hear anyone mention giving to someone who is less fortunate, a person we might not even know, or giving something to Jesus for His birthday? Unfortunately, those things are hardly ever mentioned, even in our churches.

As you examine the holiday traditions of your family, consider this principle from Acts 20:35: "It is more blessed to give than receive." These words are attributed to Jesus by Luke, the author of the book of Acts, yet they are not recorded in the Gospels. Obviously, not all of Jesus' words were written down (see John 21:25), thus this saying must have been passed on orally through the apostles. The principle here is very important to the way we should observe Christmas: The focus of your family's Christmas celebration should be on giving, not getting. There is nothing wrong with exchanging presents with business associates or those you care about but what about making it a tradition to give to those in need? And what if your family made it a priority to give something special back to Jesus each Christmas? This is an important principle for children to learn at an early age, and for parents to practice each holiday season. Look for ways to keep this kind of biblical giving a central focus of your family Christmas traditions.

Fourth, *be aware of the spiritual struggle* that can take place at Christmas. One of Satan's most effective strategies—and therefore a great danger to believers—is the deception that there is no serious conflict between good and evil in our world. Some would even argue things appear to be getting better and better. But the Bible is clear that the war between God and Satan has not diminished but instead has intensified, including its conflict on this earth.

In Ephesians 6, Paul reminds his readers that the Christian struggle is not only against Satan but also against a host of his subordinates, who like the devil himself are not flesh and blood. They are not mere fantasies, but are very real. Our greatest enemy is not the world we see, corrupt and wicked as it is, but the world we cannot see. The devil seems to be most effective when he carries out his strategies subtly, therefore I am convinced that his number one target today is young people. He recognizes that the earlier he can capture their attention, the more of their lives he can influence.

Keeping Christ out of Christmas is part of Satan's strategy. He doesn't care how we celebrate the holiday as long as Jesus is not the main focus of our attention. If the devil can keep Christ out of our Christmas, he's got a foothold by which he can subtly influence our thinking in other dimensions of life. Of course, any self-respecting Christian would be quick to respond with, "Jesus is part of my Christmas holiday!" Yet the real question we have to ask ourselves is if the Lord is merely a part of our celebration or if He is the reason for the season.

This Christmas, keep in mind the spiritual struggle going on in our world. Each time you feel yourself losing sight of the "reason for the season," repeat 2 Corinthians 9:15 to yourself: "Thanks be to God for His indescribable gift!" It's just enough to refocus your thoughts and keep your mind on the real reason we can celebrate Christmas.

Fifth, remember *to give God first place at Christmas,* and you'll find it easier to do the same the other 364 days of the year. This biblical truth is outlined for us in Matthew 6:33: "But seek first his kingdom and his righteousness, and all these things will be given to you as well."

To give God first place in your life means to turn to Him first for help, to take His life for your pattern of living, to fill your thoughts with His desires and to obey Him in everything. People, goals, objects, and other desires all compete for priority in your life. Any of these can bump God out of first place if you don't actively choose to give Him primacy in every area of your life.

The phrase "What would Jesus do?" became extremely popular in the last half of the '90s, especially among young people. For the sake of our discussion in this book, let's change the question to "What would Jesus do at Christmastime?" This simple little phrase could have a profound effect on the way we observe the season this year.

Ultimately, the goal of our Christmas celebration should be to give God glory. First Corinthians 10:31 summarizes it this way: *"So whether you eat or drink or whatever you do, do it all for the glory of God."*

8

Parenting in a Consumer Culture

I t is December. The stores are jammed with shoppers buying presents. Cash registers are ringing. The merchants are wrapping gifts and sending customers through the doors loaded down with packages. Welcome to our consumer culture.

We have a generation of young people who are consuming things at such a rapid pace that they are not only unaware of what they are devouring but also are failing to appreciate all that they possess. Unfortunately, Christmas more than any other time of the year feeds this frenzy.

I remember my own struggles with Christmas consumerism as a child. My brother Victor, sister Cindy, and I could hardly wait for Christmas morning to come. Our imaginations ran wild with anticipation of all that would be waiting for us under the tree. My parents had devised a plan by which they could securely hide all our presents until Christmas morning, without the possibility of our finding them. By Christmas Eve, it was all we could do to contain our excitement.

By three o'clock in the morning we were wide awake and couldn't go back to sleep no matter how hard we tried—if in fact we had slept at all! We made our way across the house to our parents' bedroom and banged on the door. "Go to sleep," my father bellowed. "It's three o'clock in the morning!" We'd wait a while, then attempt to rouse our parents at least three more times before they finally warned us that there would be no gifts at all if we tried to wake them again before seven o'clock.

That's when we began our marathon Monopoly game. Why Monopoly—who knows? Let's just say it kept us occupied until that most important time when the clock struck seven. Then nothing was going to stop us from our rendezvous with presents. After we had secured our personal stash of gifts, we would tear through the wrapping paper at the speed of light, tossing presents in a pile behind us. No sooner did we finish opening all our gifts than the three of us cried out in unison those all-too-familiar words, "Is that all there is?" It was Christmas consumerism at its best.

Remembering the reason for the season is just one of the many current issues that demands strong and thoughtful parental guidance. It's not easy being a mom or dad today, and everyone knows that parenting is risky business. There are no money-back guarantees that all will turn out well for our kids. However, God does promise us in Proverbs 22:6 that if we "point our kids in the right direction, when they're old, they won't be lost" (TM). The key to raising healthy kids in a consumer culture is to take God's Word seriously and apply it to every dimension of life. It's practical, timely, and relevant to all the issues of life, including how to keep Christ in Christmas.

What's Your Communication Style?

One of the greatest problems families face today is a lack of healthy communication. It is an ever-increasing cause for frustration among kids and parents alike. Clear, loving communication in your family is imperative for balanced living in a consumer culture.

Lawrence Richards has provided a helpful explanation of parent-child communication. Drawing from the work of Ross Snyder, Richards characterizes four levels of parental response through the following illustration:[23] A child in a boat is headed for certain disaster. He obviously made a bad decision upstream. His parent will respond in one of four ways. The *advice-giver* is far removed from the emotional crisis. He hollers, "Row harder! Why did you get into the water in the first place? What a stupid kid! I told you not to do it. Didn't you read the warning signs?" The *reassurer* is closer to the situation and responds, "You were a good kid. Your mother and I love you. Of the last three people who went over the falls, two survived. Good luck!" The *understander* steps into the water and says, "Hey, the current is very strong here. You really are in trouble, aren't you? Let me see if I can get you some help." The *self-revealer* gets into the boat with the child and immediately starts paddling to safety.

In our book *The Seduction of Our Children,*[24] Neil Anderson and I cited another example of parent-child communication. Suppose your child comes home from school with sorrow written all over his face. You ask him what's wrong, and he tells you that his best friend has rejected him. How do you respond?

If you are an advice-giver you might say something like, "I never did like that kid anyway. What did you do to make him reject you? Next time be more careful about choosing your friends. I think what you need to do is..."

If you are a reassurer, you will probably wrap your arms around him and say, "Your mother and I love you. You're a good kid, and I know you will survive this crisis. You'll find another friend."

If you are an understander, you might respond, "Hey, that hurts doesn't it? Can we sit down and talk about it? Can you share with me what happened?"

But if you're a self-revealer, you will give the child a hug and sit quietly with him for a moment reflecting on a time you were rejected. Then you may respond, "Two years ago my best friend turned his back on me. I trusted him as much as I trusted anyone. It was one of the most painful experiences of my life. I sense you are going through the same thing I did."

We have asked hundreds of teenagers to identify how their parents respond to similar situations. Ninety-five percent identified their parents as advice-givers. Five percent said their parents were reassurers. Not one teenager identified his parents as under-standers or self-revealers. I'm not saying that you don't need to give advice and offer reassurance to your child, nor is any one response appropriate in every situation. But a serious communi-cation problem exists when kids report that their parents respond almost exclusively with advice-giving and reassurance.

When your child is hurt or in trouble, he needs a self-revealer to get into the boat with him. If you don't adopt this communi-cation style, your child may eventually be the victim of an even greater disaster. We should all strive to be the kind of parent a son or daughter can come to and confide in. If our kids know that we will respond to them with love, trust, and respect for them no matter what they tell us, they will open up like flowers to a warm sun.

Get in Touch with Your Kids

All too frequently I find that parents know more about their ancestral history than they do about the activities of their chil-dren. An important element of parenting is getting a grasp of the likes, dislikes, and lifestyle of your kids. This can only happen when a conscious effort is made to invade their world and encounter their culture. Without this "hands-on" knowledge, it's tough to *earn* the right to be heard and talk with your children. In our position as parents, we can attempt to *enforce* the right to be heard, but it's not nearly as effective.

In 1 Corinthians 9:22 we find some advice that can be applied to this very element of parenting: "When I am with those whose consciences bother them easily, I don't act as though I know it all and don't say they are foolish; the result is that they are willing to let me help them. Yes, whatever a person is like, I try to find common ground with him so that he will let me tell him about Christ and let Christ save him" (TLB). The apostle Paul gives sev-eral important principles for parenting: Establish common ground with your kids, avoid a know-it-all attitude, learn from your kids about their world, let your kids know that you accept them, be sensitive to their needs and concerns, and—most important—look for opportunities to live out and share your faith with them.

I encourage you to learn to listen to your children. Kids today need their parents to do more than just "hear them out"—they need moms and dads who will listen to them. Webster's Dictionary defines "listening" as "to hear with thoughtful attention." Ask yourself, when was the last time you gave thoughtful attention to your son or daughter?

Proverbs 18:13 says, "Answering before listening is both stupid and rude" (TM). Sometimes it is easy to advise or correct your children in a given situation before you have really heard *with thoughtful attention* what they have to say. This takes time and work, but it beats acting like the person who says, "Don't confuse me with the facts!"

James 1:19 offers this advice for parenting: "Everyone should be quick to listen, slow to speak and slow to become angry" (NIV). This verse encourages parents to put a mental stopwatch on their conversations and keep track of how much they talk and how much they listen. Listening demonstrates to our kids that we think what they have to say is important. If you want to shape their thinking about Christmas, be willing to both talk and listen.

Work at Understanding Your Child

Do you really comprehend the challenges your kids are facing today—especially the older ones? Forty percent of kids surveyed said that their views are either ignored or bypassed by their parents. Consequently, they conclude that their parents don't really care about them or their ideas. Our ability to grasp their outlook about different issues in life enables us to better demonstrate our care and concern for them. Learning to understand is foundational to positive relationships. We must become thoroughly familiar with the personality and disposition of our children, and we must work at putting ourselves in the position of our children in order to gain more insight about the world in which they live.

Things are markedly different today from when we grew up. Certainly there are similar problems as with previous generations, such as drug and alcohol abuse, premarital sex, and rebellion. However, the problems facing kids today are more complex and more intense than in any previous generation. That's why it is important for parents today to put themselves in their children's place. A lot of the strain between parents and kids nowadays could be reduced through better communication and understanding. It's been said that home is not where you live but where you are understood.

Proverbs 11:12 reminds us that "a person of understanding holds his tongue." How many times have you said something that you regret right after the words roll off your tongue? Imagine how different family life might be if we as parents worked harder at understanding our children and their perspectives before we spoke. According to Proverbs 13:15, good understanding wins favor. Gaining favor through understanding with our children can help us navigate a multitude of child-rearing issues.

I think every parent should seek to understand their kids, and serve as a source of encouragement. We all need encouragement. Our world is not a very encouraging place to live. Despair, resentment, and disillusionment enshroud this generation. That's why it is so important for our homes to be places of hope and help. Kids need a safe refuge where they are sure someone cares and wants the best for them.

Encouragement is an important principle woven throughout the New Testament. First Thessalonians 5:11 reads, "Therefore encourage one another and build each other up, just as in fact you are doing" (NIV). Life is a marathon. There are times when your feet ache, your throat burns, and your whole body cries out for you to stop. This is when you need to have supporters, people who believe in you. Their encouragement helps to push you along and motivates you to hang in there. In the same way, Christians are to encourage one another. This is especially true for parents with their children. A word of encouragement offered at just the right time can be the difference between continuing to run the race of life and collapsing along the way. Look around your home. Be sensitive to the need for encouragement that other family members may have and then offer supportive words or actions.

Love Them Genuinely

Everyone believes love is important, but we usually think of love as a feeling, when in reality genuine love is a choice and an action. First Corinthians 13:4-7 puts it this way: "Love is very patient and kind, never jealous or envious, never boastful or proud, never haughty or selfish or rude. Love does not demand its own way. It is not irritable or touchy. It does not hold grudges and will hardly even notice when others do it wrong. It is never glad about injustice, but rejoices whenever truth wins out. If you love someone you will be loyal to him no matter what the cost. You will always believe in him, and always stand your ground in defending him." (TLB)

These verses offer us a great checklist to examine the kind of love we demonstrate toward other members of our family. Our kids need this kind of love if they are going to survive in a consumer culture. However, the kind of love the Bible is talking about is not humanly possible without the Lord's help. God is the source of our love. He loved us enough to sacrifice His only Son for us, taking the punishment for our sins. Jesus is the ultimate example of what it means to love. Everything He did in life and death was supremely loving. The Holy Spirit gives us the power to love. God's love always involves a choice and an action, and our love for our children should be just like His.

The bottom line is that parenting is never easy. It takes time, energy, and effort. In the last twenty years we've seen increased spending on education and social welfare. Parents are better educated and families are smaller, yet our children are at greater risk than ever before. Why? A major contributing factor is a generation of parents who are unwilling to spend time building into the lives of their children. There is no substitute for sharing our lives with our kids. After all, most kids today spell love "T-I-M-E." A simple way to stay in touch with your kids and spend time with them is to make sure that you have at least one meal per day as a family. Sit together around the table and make sure that the television set is switched off. Meals can be a great time to connect as a family and find out about each member's activities for the day. The concept of having a meal together may be new to your family, but it is definitely worth making a priority in your home.

Ultimately, if we want our children to survive in this consumer age, we must not only spend time building into their lives but also help them develop a vital, personal relationship with Jesus Christ, the ultimate Christmas gift. He is our strength, hope, and peace in a confused world that has lost its way. Don't assume your child is a Christian simply because you are a Christian and have taken him to Sunday school on a regular basis. Each person must personally receive Jesus Christ as Savior and Lord, and who better to lead him to that commitment than his parent? *Pray for your child's salvation.* You can't argue your children into becoming Christians, but you can pray for them and allow God to prepare their hearts to receive the Gospel. Your child's salvation should be at the top of your prayer list.

Also, tell them stories. Kids often understand concepts better when they are presented through stories. Tell or read your child Bible stories about people who were challenged to surrender their lives to Christ. You might consider using the example of Jesus talking with Nicodemus (John 3) or Zacchaeus (Luke 19). Expose your child to good Christian children's books that present God's love and plan of salvation.

At some point you must clearly and lovingly share the Gospel with your child and invite him or her to receive Christ. There are many excellent tracts available that summarize the Gospel in terms a child can understand. Whether you use one of these tools or not, your presentation should include these basic truths:

• God loves you and wants to give you peace and abundant life (John 3:16, 10:10; Romans 5:1).

- You are sinful and separated from God (Romans 3:23; 6:23).

- Jesus paid the penalty for your sin when He died on the cross (John 14:6; Romans 5:8).

- You must confess your sin and receive Jesus Christ as Savior and Lord (John 1:12; 1 John 1:9; Revelation 3:20).

As you talk with your child about spiritual matters, be sure to speak at his level. Don't use "Christianese" or abstract theological terms ("saved," "justification," etc.) without thoroughly explaining their meaning in words your child can understand. Also, don't try to scare or manipulate your child into making a response. Simply present the Gospel, answer his or her questions, and allow the Holy Spirit to bring him or her to the point of deciding to receive Christ.

After you have explained the plan of salvation and are convinced that your child understands it, give a clear invitation. Say something like, "Would you like to receive Jesus right now?" If he responds negatively, accept his decision and continue to pray for him and share the Gospel with him in the future. If he says yes, lead him in a simple prayer by having him read it aloud or repeat it after you phrase by phrase. Here is a sample prayer you can use: "Dear Jesus, I know that I have sinned and need Your forgiveness. I now turn from my sins to follow You. I believe that You died on the cross to take the punishment for my sins, and that You came back to life after three days. I invite You to come into my heart and life. I want You to be my Savior and Lord. Thank You for Your love and the gift of eternal life. In Your name I pray. Amen."

Next, review his or her decision. After leading your child in a prayer of salvation, take a few minutes to help him or her understand what has happened. What did they do? What did Christ do when they prayed? Where is Jesus right now? Make sure your child grasps the fact that he or she is now a child of God.

Of course, it's possible that you have been reading about leading your child to Christ but have not received the Lord as your personal Savior. Jesus died for adults as well as children. Have you come to the place in your life where you recognize that you cannot make it on your own? If you have never surrendered your life to Christ, why not take a few minutes right now to pray the simple prayer suggested above? Receiving Christ is the most important thing you will ever do. There's no greater joy than knowing God personally. Once you've made the decision to follow Jesus, Christmas takes on a whole new meaning.[25]

If you or your child receive Christ as a result of this publication, please contact our ministry using the information in the back of the book. We'd like to pray with you and send you some information on how to begin this new relationship with Jesus.

9

How to Keep Christ in Christmas

C hristmas is supposed to be the most joyous time of the year, yet a darkening anxiety can easily enshroud our activities. In households throughout the country, adults feverishly plan the greatest Christmas ever for their family members and friends. With each passing day they grow weary of the unending list of gifts to buy, social functions to attend, and lavish meals to prepare, plus the relentless "I wants" coming from their children. They worry that their best efforts at orchestrating the holiday events will fall short, and they realize too late that they are spending way beyond their means.

Many people today are looking for a way to leave this holiday treadmill. One frazzled parent, exasperated by the demands of the season, confessed that "the holidays depress me so much, just thinking about the coming month makes me want to leave town." Another said, "Everything about it—shopping for gifts, wrapping, making the holiday meals and treats, decorating the house —just makes me feel tired. Sometimes it seems like there's no point to so much festivity. Sure, my kids probably would feel left out if we didn't do what their friend's families did, but otherwise, what's the point?" Can you relate? Do you ever find yourself with similar feelings at Christmastime?

There are healthy alternatives to this stress-filled ritual, better ways to celebrate the "reason for the season." However, you must determine that it is time for a change, then develop a plan to make the necessary changes to establish a balance that is both fun and appropriate for your family. And it's best to put this plan together early in the fall, so as not to be swept away in the all-too-typical holiday confusion.

Family Traditions

Developing special traditions is an important element of having a healthy family. Christmas is a great time to acquire enjoyable, meaningful holiday practices that will provide fond memories in the lives of parents and kids alike. In such a highly mobile society, and with the fracturing of so many families today, special traditions can help give children a sense of security as they look forward to certain practices each holiday season. These traditions also can help to deepen their faith from a practical aspect, as they have the opportunity to celebrate the birth of Christ.

Ever since our twins were infants, my wife and I have made an effort to form meaningful traditions for our family at Christmastime. Now our youngest daughter is also sharing in these family holiday practices. Here's a rundown of some of the Christmas traditions we practice each year to help keep our family focused on keeping Christ in Christmas. Maybe these will give you some ideas of things your family can do.

Each year at Christmastime we visit a local candy store for a demonstration of how candy canes are made. Jerry at Logan's Candy Shop in Ontario, California, is one of the few remaining craftsmen in the country who still makes candy canes by hand. We've been going for so many years now, I feel like I could provide the dialogue for the demonstration! But our family never gets tired of watching Jerry and his faithful crew produce a batch of candy canes from scratch. (Our favorite part is when they hand out samples that are still warm!) And we rarely leave without purchasing some candy cane ice cream for a treat at home later on.

Often we invite another family to go with us to the demonstration. After we watch the candy canes being made, we take a few minutes to walk down Euclid Avenue in downtown Ontario and look at a series of lighted displays depicting key events in the life of Christ.

Every year we like to plan a birthday party for Jesus. This does not necessarily have to be held on Christmas Day, however it seems to take on more meaning when it's as close to that day as possible. Make a cake and have family members help decorate it. And don't forget to decorate for the party with festive streamers, napkins, and the like.

Prior to the party, discuss what special gift each person is planning to give Jesus. Take time at the party to sing "Happy Birthday" to Jesus, and have each family member share the present they are giving Him.

Find out where special holiday light displays are located in your community, then visit them some evening. We've discovered several neighborhoods that have superb light displays in our area and it usually takes us two or three nights to visit them all. Sometimes we drive; other times, we bundle up in warm clothing and walk around the streets, enjoying the sights and sounds of Christmas.

Many churches in southern California have special Christmas events open to the public. First Baptist Church in Yucaipa presents a magnificent production called "Bethlehem Marketplace"— an all-encompassing tour utilizing drama, music, and live animals. You make your way through a mock-up of ancient Bethlehem at the time of Christ's birth. The sets, smells, music, and actors seem to transport you back to that very first Christmas. At the end of your tour there is a clear Gospel presentation and an opportunity for people to receive Christ. This is a holiday favorite of our clan, and we often invite friends and relatives to attend with us.

Another favorite tradition for our family is to attend the special dinner and musical creation at Eagle Rock Baptist Church. The holiday musical production is different each year and is packed with top-quality music and drama, and well-designed sets. Each presentation begins with a delicious meal and concludes with a clear explanation of the "reason for the season." This has become a yearly tradition not just for our immediate family but for our extended family as well.

Another church in our area hosts an "angel breakfast" each year. The morning is designed specifically for preschoolers. The first thing they do upon arrival is to make a Christmas craft. Then everyone comes together and breakfast is served. The meal is designed to delight the taste buds of a preschooler: Fruit Loops, donut holes, mini-muffins, and sliced bananas were served one year. While the children and adults are eating, dry ice is placed strategically around the room to simulate clouds. Then a choir of angels (usually fathers and grandfathers) sing a couple Christmas carols. After their brief "performance," each angel visits one of the tables and tells the children the significance of the Christmas story. Each child then receives an angel ornament to take home.

In early December our family has adopted the European tradition of placing a shoe at the foot of the bed before we go to sleep. Tradition says that on December 6, Father Christmas visits each house and leaves a gift in your shoe, based on your behavior from the past year. If you've been good, you receive a piece of fruit. If you've been bad, you receive a rock. We've had some fun with this in our family, and it can easily lead into a discussion of what kind of behavior pleases God and how He rewards us.

As a family, we have also established the tradition of watching our collection of Christmas videos each year. We start right after Thanksgiving and go through the assortment of classics, watching everything from "How the Grinch Stole Christmas" to "It's a Wonderful Life." This has become a time for our family to relax and be together. These films also provide a basis for some interesting discussions on what each one actually says about Christmas. Some contain strong underlying Christian themes.

Our family enjoys reading a variety of books and short stories together during the holidays. There are a number of good Christmas books and stories that are great for all ages to enjoy. Some of our favorites include *Christ in Christmas: A Family Advent Celebration*, by NavPress Publishers; *Santa and the Christ Child*, by Nicholas Bakewell; *Santa, Are You for Real?*, by Harold Myra; *The Christmas Stories of George McDonald*, by David C. Cook Publishers; and *The Night Before Christmas*, by Clement Moore.

As you can see, we have found a multitude of things to do as a family during the holiday season. Some things are just for fun, and others allow for spiritual input. You are only limited by time and imagination. However, when you make a concerted effort, each situation can become part of family tradition and offer another opportunity to celebrate the birth of Jesus.

Spread the Joy

There is no better time to tell others the great news about Jesus than Christmas. Many people seem to be more receptive to spiritual things, while others are desperately searching for ways to overcome their pain and loneliness. Statistically, in spite of all the parties and festivities, there are more suicides at Christmas than at any other time of the year.

The apostle Paul reminds us in 2 Corinthians 5:20 that we are "Christ's ambassadors." Christmas offers us numerous opportunities to fulfill this biblical responsibility: in our families, on our campuses, in our neighborhoods, and in the world. We should approach each day of the holiday season with prayerful attention to those we may come in contact with who need a relationship with God, then carefully and thoughtfully share the message of Christmas with them. Sometimes these opportunities come to us personally, while other times the Lord opens doors for us to take the message of Christmas to others in different situations and through a variety of organizations. In each case we are sharing the greatest Christmas gift ever—Jesus!

Every Christmas, for many years, our family has been part of a special evangelistic outreach to male juvenile offenders incarcerated in southern California. This outreach was started by some dear friends, Frank and Edie Johnston, more than 50 years ago.

We became part of the ministry team when I served as a youth pastor, and we have continued to participate every year since. This past year, we added an additional facility to our route.

The special evening outreach, in each facility, includes a number of elements. Our team of volunteers puts together a special program that includes a band, special music, Christmas carols, and refreshments. Each year we also try to include some special entertainment that we think the boys at the facility will enjoy. One year a friend brought a group of men to put on a martial arts demonstration. This past year I brought one of the comedians from our *Real Answers* team with us. I complete the evening's program with a drum solo and a Gospel presentation. My family also joins me in this outreach, helping to serve the refreshments and pass out Bibles and literature as the boys leave the gym to go back to their dorms. This has proved a wonderful opportunity for our family to bring the love and peace of Christmas to young men who will otherwise spend a lonely holiday locked up. We also get to share in the joy of serving together and seeing people receive Christ.

Operation Christmas Child is a project of Samaritan's Purse, headed by Franklin Graham. Shoe boxes are filled with small gifts, along with portions of Scripture, and then distributed to poor children around the world. Last year more than two million shoe boxes were distributed to children in more than 50 countries. We have found that participating in Operation Christmas Child gives the family an opportunity to work on a small project together. As you fill the box with various items, it gives you a chance to share the Gospel and know you are making an eternal difference in a child's life. If you would like to make Operation Christmas Child part of your family's outreach, you can contact Samaritan's Purse online at http://www.samaritan.org .

Angel Tree is a ministry of Prison Fellowship, founded by Chuck Colson. This is a unique Christmas outreach project to the children of prisoners, and mobilizes nearly 15,000 churches each year across the country. Prison Fellowship staff members publicize Angel Tree inside prisons, and inmates sign their children up for Christmas gifts, which are given (in the incarcerated parent's name) by generous churches and volunteers. Paper angels are provided by Prison Fellowship to be placed on a Christmas tree in your church. Each angel contains the age and sex of a child, as well as guidelines for purchasing an appropriate gift. You then have the opportunity to "adopt" an angel and purchase a gift for him or her. The gifts are collected and delivered by a Prison Fellowship volunteer sometime before Christmas. What makes this program unique is that the presents and the Gospel are given in the name of the incarcerated parent. Angel Tree is designed to brighten children's Christmas and ease the pain of separation. You can contact Prison Fellowship at 1-800-398-HOPE, or write to them at Angel Tree, P.O. Box 17500, Washington, DC 20041-0500.

The Advent Season

Losing the sense of wonder and excitement of preparing to celebrate the coming of Jesus has become all too common. And it's easy to forget that for our children, the days are long and the waiting is hard until December 25! But that's what the season of Advent is all about—waiting and preparing for the birth of Jesus Christ. Advent is one of the simplest and most meaningful ways for your family to focus on the joyous message of Christmas. It has become a tradition in the Russo home, and I hope your family will consider making it part of your family's Christmas celebration as well.

Advent refers to the "coming" or "arrival" of Jesus Christ. The term "Advent" has several meanings within the Church: the coming of the Lord in the flesh at Christmas; His arrival in Word and Spirit; and the final Advent when Jesus will return bodily in glory. Each one gives joyful anticipation of what God has accomplished and will ultimately bring to completion.

When the church began to observe Christmas in the fourth century, a time of preparation was added. The length of time varied from three to seven weeks. In the tenth century, an agreement was reached in the Western world that Advent should consist of four Sundays. The first Sunday of Advent occurs on or near November 30. While always including four Sundays, the season may vary in length from twenty-two days to twenty-eight days, always ending on Christmas Eve.

An Advent celebration will require dedication and some sacrifice. Priorities will have to change so you can focus on what is important. Set aside some time on your calendar ahead of time and protect it. Then turn off the TV and turn on the answering machine for the brief time it takes. Make sure the rest of your family realizes that this is an important family moment.

Many Christians find the preparation and use of an Advent wreath to be meaningful. During each Sunday's observance of Advent, a candle is lit. On Christmas Eve, all five candles are lit. The bright light provides a great climax to the weeks of preparation and personifies the Light of the World that was illumined centuries ago with the first cry of the Christ child.

Your wreath can be as simple or lavish as you desire. Basically, it is a wreath with five inserted candles—some use four red or purple candles and one white "Christ candle." For centuries the wreath has been made from fresh-cut greenery—pine, laurel, holly, bayberry, or any other evergreen shrub or tree. Additional decoration, available from craft shops or made at home, can bring extra beauty to your wreath.

For example, cut five small X's in an inverted pie tin, then poke the five candles through. Garnish the pie tin with pine branches. You can also use a Styrofoam ring as a foundation, then gently press the candles into it. Decorate the ring with holly, evergreen branches, pine cones, ornaments, or whatever you choose.

Our family found a small, round ceramic evergreen tree that works great. It is white, with a wide ring around the bottom and five spots for candles. These can generally be found in Christmas supply or craft stores. Some people use a grapevine wreath, with five slender candles. Others have cut a wooden ring to utilize each year. By drilling five holes, they can dress it up with a variety of decorations.

Try to make this process a family activity and have fun! Place the completed wreath in a location where it has central focus but won't have to be moved. A counter top, dining room table, or mantel are all possibilities. Remember to be careful when the candles are lit. Dry greenery can be a fire hazard. Make sure each member of the family is aware of the potential danger.

Week One: The Prophecy Candle

Gather your family together and light the first colored candle of the wreath. Either Mom or Dad will say, "Our circle of light begins. We have to wait four weeks for Christmas day to come and that can seem like a long time. However, the people before Jesus was born waited hundreds of years for God to do what He promised He would do—send Jesus to be our Savior. They must have felt like giving up many times, wondering if God would ever fulfill His promise. The Old Testament prophet Isaiah wrote about God's promise."

Then ask someone to read Isaiah 7:14; 9:2,6, and 7, before going on to say, "God promised that He would send Jesus to save us from our sins. We call the first candle, the 'Prophecy Candle' to remind us of God's wonderful promise. Can you remember any other promises that God has made to us in the Bible? (Allow time for discussion.) Remember, God always keeps His promises."

Next, read Matthew 1:21-23, then remind everyone, "This promise did come to be, and His name was Jesus. The Bible tells us of another great name that was given to Jesus: 'Immanuel' which means 'God with us'." Sing together the old favorite, "O Come, O Come, Emmanuel," then join hands around the Advent wreath and pray together, thanking God for the many promises in His Word.

To close this first night's Advent celebration, make a family Christmas card list together. Have each person think about special people in their lives and add them to the list. Once the list is complete, make a container to hold the Christmas cards you will receive. The container could be something ready-made, like a basket that you decorate, or it could be something that is designed and crafted by family members and then decorated. Use your imagination and have fun. Choose three cards each day when you gather together for Advent, and pray for those families.

During the week, light the first candle and read the following verses. Briefly discuss each passage and follow each day's reading with a time of family prayer.

Monday: Genesis 1:26-31
Tuesday: Genesis 3:1-24
Wednesday: Genesis 3:15
Thursday: Deuteronomy 18:15-19
Friday: Isaiah 7:10-14
Saturday: Isaiah 11:1-5

Week Two: The Bethlehem Candle

Gather your family together, light the first *and* second candles and say, "The candle we light today is a reminder of the preparation that was made for the coming of the Savior Jesus. The promise of God made it clear just exactly where Jesus would be born." Read Micah 5:2 and Luke 2:1-7, then remind everyone that the second candle is called the Bethlehem Candle. This was part of God's special plan concerning the birth of His Son—a plan that was prophesied 400 years earlier. Considering there was so much advance notice, it seems like the town would have been prepared for such an important event. There should have been some kind of welcoming committee for Mary and Joseph, to take care of the needs of this couple and the special baby about to be born. But none of this happened. The town was so consumed with activity and filled with people and that it missed the birth of the Savior.

Sing together "O Little Town of Bethlehem," then join hands around the Advent wreath and offer a prayer of thanks to God for the precious gift of His Son.

For your family activity, give each member of the family a light (such as a flashlight or candle), then turn out all the lights in the house. Ask everyone to walk around in the darkness for a moment, to experience what the darkness is like. Next, turn on your lights and ask your family, "How did you feel walking around in darkness? (Remember, darkness in the Bible is used as a symbol of life without Jesus.) Was your light very helpful? (Light is a symbol of Jesus and being able to 'see' things clearly.) How much light does it take to overcome the darkness? (True light is found in Jesus Christ—the Light of the World.)"

During the week, light the first and second candles and read the following verses. Then briefly discuss each passage and follow the day's reading with a time of family prayer.

Monday: Isaiah 19:19-25
Tuesday: Isaiah 40:9-11
Wednesday: Isaiah 42:1-4
Thursday: Isaiah 49:1-7
Friday: Isaiah 53:1-12
Saturday: Isaiah 61:1-3

Week Three: The Angel's Candle

Gather your family together and light the first, second, and third candles of the Advent wreath. Say to them, "What would it be like if you were gazing at the stars one peaceful night and the sky suddenly exploded with hundreds of angels singing praises to God? That's what happened, many years ago, the night the 'Good News of Great Joy' was brought to all the people. This week's candle represents the angel and the fantastic message of the birth of Jesus."

Have someone read Luke 2:8-14, then remind them that there were no announcement cards sent out when Jesus was born.

Instead, an angel announced the wonderful news. The angel came to Bethlehem that night to announce the most incredible event in human history. God's greatest gift ever had come to earth. Read 2 Corinthians 9:15, then sing together "O Come, All Ye Faithful." Join hands around the Advent wreath and thank God for the good news of great joy.

For your family activity, give each person a piece of paper and something to draw with (crayons or colored pencils). Have everyone create their own birth announcement for Jesus. Encourage each person to be creative and think about what an announcement might look like if you were to buy one at the "Bethlehem Hallmark" store. Ask each person to explain their design, then share ideas about different ways to tell others the good news about Jesus.

During the week, light the first three candles on the Advent wreath and read the following verses. Briefly discuss each passage and follow each day's reading with a time of family prayer.

Monday: Jeremiah 23:5-6
Tuesday: Micah 5:2
Wednesday: Zechariah 9:9-10
Thursday: Malachi 3:1
Friday: Luke 1:1-25
Saturday: Luke 1:26-38

Week Four: The Shepherd's Candle

Once your family has gathered together, light the first, second, third, and fourth candles of the Advent wreath. Say to them, "The circle of light is almost complete. The waiting is almost over. God is faithful, and the Son has been born. It is important that we reflect the 'Light of the World' in our daily lives, as we share the Good News." Read Luke 2:8-20, then tell them, "The fourth candle represents the shepherds. They were excited about all they had heard and seen about Jesus! Suppose that you were one of those shepherds—how would you have responded?" Take a few minutes to let your children share their responses, then read Matthew 1:18-25.

Gather around the Advent wreath, holding hands. Sing "Silent Night," then offer prayers of praise to God for His wonderful gift.

For your family activity, read Matthew 2:1-12 and hand out paper bags and crayons to make puppets based on the people in the passage you just read. Have each person select their puppet character, assign one member of the family to write a script and read it, and ask other members to act out the dialogue with their puppets. Finish by discussing the difference between the shepherds' response and that of everyone else in Bethlehem.

During the week, light the first four candles on the Advent wreath and read the following verses. Briefly discuss each passage and follow each day's reading with a time of family prayer.

Monday: Luke 1:39-56
Tuesday: Luke 2:1-20
Wednesday: Luke 2:21-38
Thursday: Colossians 1:15-23
Friday: Revelation 5:1-14
Saturday: Revelation 21:1-7

Christmas Eve or Christmas Day: Christ's Candle

Gather the family together and light all five of the candles on the Advent wreath. Remind everyone, "Christmas is a time to show love. Our love for others, our love for God, and His wonderful love for us." Read 1 John 4:9-10, and say, "We greet your coming, Lord Jesus, with love and amazement. As a family we declare, 'Joy to the world—the Lord has come!'" Next, read Luke 1:68-69 and sing together that wonderful Christmas hymn, "Joy to the World."

Hold hands as you gather around the Advent wreath. Thank God for His care and concern for every detail of your family's life, and ask Him to bring joy to your house today as you celebrate the Messiah's birth.

For your family activity, write the name of each family member on a piece of paper, fold it, and put the papers together in a jar. Have each person draw a name from the container (if you pick your own, return it, folded, to the container and draw another one). For the person whose name you draw, share a few thoughts about what you appreciate about them. If possible, write these things down. This "gift" will become a reminder of why Christ came that very first Christmas. Close by reading Luke 1:67-69, and asking your children, "What gift did Jesus bring to us on His first coming?"

It's All Up to You

Keeping Christ in Christmas is no easy task, but it doesn't have to be filled with frenzied activity and weariness. To successfully make Christmas Christ-centered for you and your family, create a plan that will have your family focused on the Lord throughout the month of December.

As Matthew 6:33 reminds us, we must give God first place in our lives and turn to Him for help and guidance in every dimension of our lives, including how we celebrate Christmas. We must fill our thoughts with His desires, make His character our pattern, and determine to obey Him. The patterns and behavior of our world can quickly bump Christ out of Christmas if we are not careful. We must actively choose to give Him first place in every area of our life, and celebrate Christmas with the Lord's birth as our central theme.

It's all up to you. No one else can keep Christ in Christmas for you and your family. It's a choice you must make, a plan you must develop. Without question it's worth all the effort it will take. Keeping Christ in Christmas will help set the pace for keeping Him in the center of your life all year long.

10

The Promise of Christmas

Have you ever attended a birthday party for someone you've never met? Or have you ever bought an expensive gift and given it to a perfect stranger? As crazy as it may seem, millions of people do this very thing every year at Christmastime. They give gifts, attend parties, and end up forgetting that the real reason for celebrating is a very special birthday—the birth of someone they don't even know.

In essence, many people have forgotten all about the host because they have become so preoccupied with the celebration itself and the exchanging of gifts. The real meaning of Christmas has been lost by much of our society.

Someone once said that Christmas is based on an exchange of gifts: the gift of God to man (His Son), and the gift of man to God (when we give our lives to Him). The ultimate gift of Christmas involves not only the virgin birth of Jesus Christ but also the cross where He died for our sins, and His resurrection, which gives us the guarantee of eternal life. The promise of this special gift was described by the prophet Isaiah some 700 years before the birth of Jesus:

> For to us a child is born, to us a son is given, and the government will be upon his shoulders. And he will be called Wonderful Counselor, Mighty God, Everlasting Father, the Prince of Peace. (Isaiah 9:6)

Christmas is about hope. The source of this hope comes from the Son who is given to us. He is the incredible foundation for our hope and joy. The Son is endowed with the highest honor and power and is able to do us an infinite amount of kindness. We cannot help but be fulfilled in Him. The Old Testament Prophet Isaiah uses four descriptive names or royal titles to reveal the Son's character and the essence of the hope that is found in Christ. Let's consider how these names relate to life in the twenty-first century.

Wonderful Counselor

Jesus is so wonderful that we cannot even begin to imagine how extraordinary and distinguished He truly is. He is wonderful because he is both God and man. Jesus is exceptional because His deeds are wonderful (Psalm 26:7), the things in His law—the Bible—are wonderful (Psalm 119:18), and His works are wonderful (Psalm 139:14). The apostle Paul describes some of these works in 1 Corinthians 2:9: "No eye has seen, no ear has heard, no mind has conceived what God has prepared for those who love him." We are not even able to comprehend all that God has in store for us, both in this life and in eternity. Knowing this should cause us to worship Him and submit to His direction for our lives.

Jesus is the supernatural counselor who, at His first coming, brought words of eternal life. When He returns for the second time, He will rule with perfect wisdom (Isaiah 11:2). Once again we turn to the encouragement of the apostle Paul:

> Oh, the depth of the riches of the wisdom and knowledge of God! How unsearchable his judgments, and his paths beyond tracing out! Who has known the mind of the Lord? Or who has been his counselor? (Romans 11:33-34).

Jesus is the authoritative One who has insight into all the issues of life. We should depend on His wisdom. Our dependence should motivate us to make Him our first resource when we need help, not our last resort.

Mighty God

Jesus not only has all wisdom; He is the One who has been given all power. He is able to do what no other can do because of His limitless power. This title is the same term applied to Yahweh in the Old Testament (Deuteronomy 10:17; Isaiah 10:21; Jeremiah 32:18), the term that predicts the ultimate victory of Jesus, the Messiah, over evil. He is strong and mighty (Psalm 24:8), serving as our mighty rock and refuge (Psalm 62:7). Knowing this should give us hope and courage to endure the hardships we experience in life. There is no problem in life that is too great for Jesus to overcome. There is no bad habit or addiction He cannot conquer. A.W. Tozer once said, "With the goodness of God to desire our highest welfare, the wisdom of God to plan it, and the power of God to achieve it, what do we lack?"

That little baby lying helpless in Mary's arms that first Christmas morning held the universe together. He has all the power necessary to transform lives and bring hope to a disillusioned heart.

Everlasting Father

The Son who is given to us is the Father of Eternity. He is the creator of all things—even time and the distant purpose of every single thing. Jesus is the author of everlasting life and happiness. The "foreverness" of Jesus, in relationship to time, is reflected in several descriptive phrases in the Old Testament. His righteousness, kindness, and kingdom are everlasting (Psalm 119:142; Isaiah 55:3; Psalm 145:13). He has promised to be our everlasting light (Isaiah 60:20). In John 8:12, Jesus said, "I am the world's light. No one who follows me stumbles around in the darkness. I provide plenty of light to live in" (TM). The evil world system in which we live is full of darkness, and its temporary overseer is the prince of darkness. By contrast, the life of Jesus gives us light so we can see the right path and avoid the enemy's pitfalls.

On the drive home from church one Sunday, when our twins Tony and Kati were younger, they were singing a song they had learned in Sunday school: *This little light of mine, I'm going to let it shine, this little light of mine, I'm going to let it shine, let it shine, let it shine, let it shine.*

The longer they sang, the more I realized that this was the "message of the season." God sent His light into a very dark world that first Christmas. No longer would darkness reign, because that little light would grow to be a man who would take away the sins of the world.

The Bible teaches that He has loved us with an everlasting love (Jeremiah 31:3). Because of His deep love for us, Jesus is eager to do the best for us, if we will only let Him. Romans 8:38 promises that nothing can ever separate us from the love of God. If we will believe this overwhelming assurance, we will not be afraid of the trials life may bring our way.

Stop for a moment and let all this soak in. God never changes. We can be assured that His righteousness, kindness, light, and love will be ours, to experience for all time. That is incredibly hard to understand because we are used to living in and dealing with a finite world. But God the Son is not bound by time or space. Jesus, the Messiah, is eternally a Father to His children. He guards them, cares for them, and supplies for all their needs. In an ever-changing world, we can feel totally secure in Christ.

Jesus is the only one who is able to bring meaning to life that goes beyond just merely existing. Life in Christ is inexhaustible and endless. It is the ultimate motivation to get out of bed in the morning and push through the challenges of life.

Prince of Peace

Jesus is the one who brings peace in the ultimate sense of the word for every dimension of life, beginning with our relationship with our heavenly Father. Individuals can know His peace, and one day the world will experience it as well. It is through Jesus that we can have peace with God (Romans 5:1). This peace we have with God differs from peaceful feelings such as confidence, assurance, and security since peace with God means that we have been restored to a right relationship with Him, a relationship that sin had severed. There is no more hostility between us: there is no sin blocking our relationship with Him. However, this peace with God is only possible because Jesus Christ paid the price for our sins with his death on the cross.

As the King, Jesus creates peace, commands peace, and preserves the peace in His kingdom. He is our peace, and it is His peace that should rule our hearts in an often confusing world. God's peace is different from the world's peace. The world usually defines peace as the absence of conflict. God's peace is confident assurance in any circumstance, no matter what the situation. With this kind of peace, we have no need to fear the present or the future. If your life is full of stress at Christmas, allow God to fill you with His true and lasting peace. Philippians 4:7 reminds us that God's peace, which surpasses all understanding, will protect your heart and mind in Christ Jesus.

Real peace comes from knowing that God is in control of every dimension of your life. As God's people we are blessed with peace (Psalm 29:11). God promises great peace to those who love His law, and the confidence that nothing can make them stumble. There can be no peace on earth, in your family, or in your heart, until Christ reigns. Jesus is the only one who can bring and maintain peace in this world.

Exchanging Gifts God's Way

In a time of great darkness, God promised to send a light that would shine on everyone living in the shadow of death. This message of hope was fulfilled in the birth of Jesus and the establishment of His eternal kingdom. God's "Gift" came to deliver all people from their slavery to sin. Sometimes it is difficult to recognize just how valuable this gift from God really is to those of us who already know the Jesus of Christmas as our Savior and Lord. Think about it for a moment. Where you would be this Christmas without Jesus? How different would your life be if you had not experienced God's ultimate Christmas gift?

At the University of Chicago Divinity School each year, they have what is called "Baptist Day." It is a day when all the Baptists in the area are invited to the school, because officials want the Baptist dollars to keep coming in. On this day each one is to bring a lunch to be eaten outdoors in a grassy picnic area. Every "Baptist Day" the school invites one of the great minds to lecture in the Theological Education Center. One year Dr. Paul Tillich was invited.

Dr. Tillich spoke for two and one-half hours, trying to prove that the resurrection of Jesus was false. He quoted scholar after scholar and book after book. He concluded that there was no such thing as the historical resurrection, therefore the religious tradition of the church was groundless, emotional, mumbo-jumbo, because it was based on a relationship with a risen Jesus, who, in fact, never rose from the dead in any literal sense. He then asked if there were any questions.

After about 30 seconds, an old, dark-skinned preacher with a head of short-cropped, woolly, white hair stood up in the back of the auditorium. "Doctor Tillich, I got a question," he said, as all eyes turned toward him. He reached into his sack lunch, pulled out an apple, and began eating it.

"Doctor Tillich..." CRUNCH, MUNCH...

"My question is a simple question." CRUNCH, MUNCH...

"Now I ain't never read them books you read..." CRUNCH, MUNCH...

"and I can't recite the Scriptures in the original Greek..." CRUNCH, MUNCH...

"I don't know nothin' about Niebuhr and Heidegger..." CRUNCH, MUNCH...

He finished his apple. "All I want to know is: this apple I just ate—was it bitter or sweet?"

Dr. Tillich paused for a moment and answered in exemplary scholarly fashion: "I cannot possibly answer that question, for I haven't tasted your apple."

The white-haired preacher dropped the core of his apple into his crumpled paper bag, then looked up at Dr. Tillich and said calmly, "Neither have you tasted my Jesus."

The 1,000-plus in attendance could not contain themselves. The auditorium erupted with applause and cheers. Dr. Tillich thanked his audience and promptly left the platform.

Have you truly tasted the Jesus of Christmas? If you have, then exchanging gifts at Christmastime should have a whole new meaning for you—an eternal meaning. As we come to grips with the significance of God's gift, it should motivate us to do all we can to help others, especially those we care about, participate in God's ultimate "gift exchange." Remember the promise of Christmas can't be bought in any store, at any price. It can only be received as a gift, and only Jesus can give it.

11

Where Do I Go From Here?

Since you've made it to this point in the book, one of two things has happened. Either you've finished this volume after diligently reading through it, or you've jumped ahead to look for an exciting conclusion! If you made the effort to faithfully read each chapter, I would like you to take a few minutes for personal reflection and application.

It would be to easy to set this book on the shelf and forget about it, but my desire is that this material would motivate you to "do something," to practically apply the information to your own situation as a concerned parent. To do this effectively will require some time on your part, but I believe it will be worth every minute invested.

Take the time to review each chapter, using the questions I have provided in this section of the book. With some chapters you will have received content that was more informative than practical. Take the time to reflect and apply anyway. In most cases I think you should be able to find at least one concept you can implement in your parenting circumstances.

If you are married, you may want to discuss these thoughts with your spouse. If you are a parent, you'll doubtless want to explore them with your kids. Invest a few moments in the study of Christmas, and you'll find a rich reward during the upcoming holiday season.

1. Christmas: In the Beginning

- What surprised you most about the history of Christmas?
- Do you recognize any remnants from ancient pagan festivals in the way Christmas is celebrated in your community?
- What were the prophecies concerning Christ's birth?

2. Santa Claus, Mistletoe, and Candy Canes

- What Christmas traditions did you practice as a child? Have you continued to carry on some of these same practices with your own children?
- How important do you feel it is to develop family traditions at Christmastime?
- What would you like to see your family do on Christmas?

3. Christmas Around the World

- What customs are practiced in the land of your ancestors?
- What are some fun things from your ethnic heritage that you could incorporate into your Christmas celebration?
- What ethnic or international activity would you like to make part of your family's holiday traditions?

4. The Christmas Rush

- How do you most frequently come in conflict with the world? What do you need to do to change this area in your life?
- Have you ever faced an incident where you were tempted to exclude God for a period of time? What happened?
- How would you describe your relationship with God? How would He describe it?

5. Whatever Happened to Christmas Vacation?

- What differences have you noticed, compared with when you were a child, in how our society observes Christmas ?

- What do you think Jesus would do with the Christmas celebration in our society?
- Describe the most unusual Christmas decoration you have ever seen. Did you like it? Why or why not?

6. Touched by an Angel

- Have you ever felt like an angel intervened in your life? What was the situation?
- Are there some examples of things that you should be doing in regard to praise and worship?
- What do we know about angels?

7. A Look at the Book

- Has your response to Christmas in the past glorified God?
- In what ways can we honor God on Christmas?
- What is the most important thing God wants us to remember about Christmas?

8. Parenting in a Consumer Age

- When was the last time you visited your child's school? How well informed are you about what takes place in the classroom?
- What do the teachers at school say about Christmas? What do some of your children's friends at school say about Christmas?
- Do you like the way your classroom is decorated? Why or why not?

9. How to Keep Christ in Christmas

- What is your favorite memory of Christmas?
- What would you like to do differently this year during the holiday season?
- What individuals, groups, or organizations would you like to help this Christmas?

10. The Promise of Christmas

- What names does Isaiah 9:6 apply to Jesus?
- How does each apply to daily life?
- Whom do you know who needs to experience God's ultimate Christmas gift in their life? How can you share this gift with that person?

A Final Word

As you continue to think about how you and your family will celebrate Christmas, try to approach the issue with as biblical a viewpoint as possible. Keep in mind that the presence of pagan elements in the early history of Christmas does not mean a Christian should automatically be disqualified from participating in some modern-day form of those elements.

Also keep in mind that many American holidays, customs, and traditions have pagan remnants in their history. It would be pretty tough to say that participating in these holidays would be wrong simply because at one time they had a pagan association. Easter is an example of a holiday that was derived from a pagan celebration, but it has become the most revered day on the Christian calendar. It is interesting to note that down through history the Church has appropriated this and other days and made them "Christian."

Even though the remnants of ancient paganism still endure, the practices and anti-Christian beliefs once associated with Christmas and other holiday customs have long since disappeared. Who would dream of not using their monthly planner because the name origins of the days of the week were originally derived from pagan gods? What would a birthday party be without a cake and candles? Can you imagine not celebrating our Lord's resurrection on Easter Sunday because of a fertility ritual? That would be crazy! So when it comes to some Christmas traditions, the way in which they were originally used should not necessarily determine our attitude towards them today.

I think our responsibility as Christians is twofold. First, we must make every effort to keep Christ in Christmas, never losing sight of the fact that Christmas is the birthday of our Savior. That is the reason we celebrate.

Second, whatever we do on or around Christmas should glorify God. We should not compromise biblical values in any way, nor should we accept the traditions of others simply because they say they are Christians. The fact that someone in your church celebrates Christmas in a particular way does not mean the traditions are right for you. Certain Christmas traditions—like Santa Claus—fall into the gray area of Christian living not specifically forbidden in the Bible. Always be aware that there will be differing opinions in the church community on how a Christian should respond to the culture, and be careful, as you exercise your Christian freedom regarding Christmas traditions, that you do not become a "stumbling block to others weaker in the faith" (I Corinthians 8:9).

Let's look for creative ways to tell others "the reason for the season." And let's do all we can to help as many as possible experience God's ultimate Christmas gift this year!

Notes

1. Everett F. Harrison, editor, *Baker's Dictionary of Theology* (Baker Book House, 1960), p. 29.
2. Clement C. Moore, *The Night Before Christmas* (Dodd, Mead & Company, 1934). Original edition published in 1848.
3. Steven Levy, "Xmas.com," *Newsweek* magazine (December 7, 1998), p. 52.
4. *U.S. News*/Bozell poll of 1,003 adults conducted by KRC Research, November 6-10, 1996.
5. Phyllis Schlafly, *Child Abuse in the Classroom* (Crossway Books, 1985), p. 11.
6. Johanna Michaelsen, *Like Lambs to the Slaughter* (Harvest House, 1989), p. 43.
7. Daniel Druckman, John A. Swets, *Enhancing Human Performance* (National Academy Press, Washington, D.C., 1988), p. 3.
8. Walter Martin, *The New Age Cult* (Bethany House Publishers, 1989), p. 63.
9. Allan Bloom, *The Closing of the American Mind* (Simon & Schuster, 1987), p. 61.
10. Russell Chandler, *Understanding the New Age* (Word, 1988), p. 154.
11. Lori Ann Pardau, Timothy A. Bittle, "What is Johnny being taught?" California Capitol Report, *Citizen* magazine (Focus on the Family, January 1990), p. 4.
12. Mel & Norma Gabler, *What Are They Teaching Our Children?* (Victor Books, 1985), p. 22.
13. Paul Vitz, *Censorship: Evidence of Bias in our Children's Textbooks* (Servant, 1986), p. 1.
14. Deborah Mendenhall, "Nightmarish Textbooks Await Your Kids," *Citizen* magazine, Focus on the Family (September 17, 1990), pp. 2-3.
15. Bob Simonds, National Association of Christian Educators, Citizens for Excellence Newsletter (May 1990), pp. 2-5.
16. William G. Sidebottom and Frank York, "They Teach New Age in New Mexico's Schools," *Citizen* magazine (July 1985), p. 10.
17. George Barna, *The Barna Report: Absolute Confusion*, (Regal Books, 1993), p. 73.
18. Nancy Gibbs, "Angels Among Us," *Time* magazine (December 29, 1993), online version.
19. Kenneth L. Woodward, "Angels: Hark! America's Latest Search for Spiritual Meaning Has a Halo Effect," *Newsweek* (December 27, 1993), pp. 52-53.
20. Ron Rhodes, *Angels Among Us* (Harvest House, 1994), pp. 29-34.

21. Billy Graham, *Angels: God's Secret Agents* (Doubleday & Company, 1975), pp. 2-3.
22. Ibid., pp. 3-4.
23. Lawrence O. Richards, *Youth Ministry* (Zondervan, 1972), pp. 139-45.
24. Neil T. Anderson and Steve Russo, *The Seduction of Our Children* (Harvest House, 1991), p. 148.

Ministry Information Page

For information on how to purchase audio and video tape resources, and other books by Steve Russo, as well as information on the *Real Answers* radio program, newletter, fact sheets, conferences, public school assemblies, and evangelistic crusades, contact:

Real Anwers with Steve Russo
P.O. Box 1549
Ontario, California 91762
(909) 466-7060
Fax (909) 466-7056

You can also visit our website at:

www.realanswers.com

Other Good
Harvest House Reading

Halloween: What's a Christian to Do?
Steve Russo

When the calendar turns to October, many Christians are faced with the yearly Halloween dilemma. As a youth evangelist and the father of three children, Steve Russo understands the problems caused by Halloween and answers your most-asked questions. Filled with practical tips on planning alternative celebrations, helpful facts on the occult and pagan festivals, and quick Bible references, this book is the ultimate one-stop reference for parents, pastors, and youth workers.

The Seduction of Our Children
Neil T. Anderson and Steve Russo

This provocative book will equip you to overcome the spiritual conflicts facing young people. It will also help you strengthen family bonds and defeat Satan's influence during these challenging days.

Squeaky Clean Jokes for Kids
Bob Phillips and Steve Russo

Authors Bob Phillips and Steve Russo scoured the country in their quest for this hilarious, wholesome entertainment! Suds will fly as kids shower their family and friends with these squeaky clean bits of wit, brilliant jokes, blazing puns, and clean-as-a-whistle knock-knocks.

Wild and Woolly Jokes for Kids
Bob Phillips and Steve Russo

Bob Phillips and Steve Russo team up again to offer the latest incredibly popular collection of wild jokes, knock-knocks, riddles, and puns.